IGOR and VERA STRAVINSKY

A PHOTOGRAPH ALBUM

1921 to 1971

Text from Stravinsky's Interviews 1912–1963

258 photographs selected by Vera Stravinsky and Rita McCaffrey

Captions by Robert Craft

THAMES AND HUDSON

Pages 1 and 2:

1 *January 1924*, St. Sylvester's Day (Russian Calendar). Brussels. Signature on a letter to Francis Poulenc. Igor drew the flower-wreath and love-bird frame.

2 *1947.* New York. Photograph by Arnold Newman.

The quotation in caption 175 on p. 102 is from John Malcolm Brinnin's *Sextet*, published in the USA in 1981 by Seymour Lawrence/Delacorte Press and in the UK in 1982 by Andre Deutsch Ltd., and appears here by kind permission of both publishers.

First published in the USA in 1982 by Thames and Hudson Inc., 500 Fifth Avenue, New York, New York 10110

Library of Congress Catalog Card Number 82-80248

Printed in Great Britain by BAS Printers, Over Wallop, Hampshire

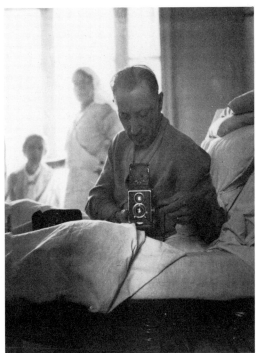

Igor and Vera Stravinsky were photographers
themselves, and perhaps the most appealing
pictures in this book are their snapshots of
each other. The chief sources are their own
albums and Mme Stravinsky's collection of
newspaper clippings, which also provide
many of the captions. The volume documents
a fifty-year love affair.

3 *March 1932*. Venice.

4 *June 1934*. Paris. In hospital after
appendectomy.

5 *1930*. Prague.

6 *November 18, 1931*. Ostend to Dover.

7 *April 1936*. Argentina.

"Belle Russe"

Anyone catching sight of Mme Vera Stravinsky as she emerges from her East Seventy-Third Street apartment building will be curious about this elderly, stooped, but regal and still beautiful woman, so different in manner and appearance from other passersby. But the striking picture that she presents is only one indication of her uniqueness, for this lady has spent most of her ninety-three years at the center of the life of music, ballet, the pictorial arts, and literature, fifty of them with the century's greatest composer. As if this were not enough, she is an artist in her own right, increasingly and justly praised as a painter.

In daily life as well as in art, one of Mme Stravinsky's most prominent characteristics is independence. The nonagenarian still makes her rounds on foot, unintimidated by the excesses of New York weather, hazards of traffic, and the mortal dangers posed by a high proportion of other inhabitants. The neighbourhood was selected for her residence because "I like to live near boutiques, as I did in Paris, and not be zoned the way you are in America." As she walks, her first destination might be the pharmacy, the bank, or Frazer-Morris, where she is permitted to taste before she buys. Or she might be headed east on Seventy-Second Street for a routine check-up with Dr. Tyson, who tells her that she is his healthiest patient. And it is true that she suffered no childhood diseases, no organic or functional disorders, has needed no operations,[1] enjoys perfect hearing and good vision, and continues, as she has done all of her life, to smoke, drink, and eat rich foods, with only very brief interludes of abstinence and dieting.

In 1920, arriving in Paris from Russia, determined to earn her own livelihood, Vera de Bosset Sudeikina began creating artificial flowers.[2] Later she took a degree in cosmetic chemistry. As she wrote to Stravinsky during his Scandinavian tour in the autumn of 1935:

I passed my chemistry exam and my professor was so pleased with me that he even had an argument with some others who didn't want to mark it "*très excellent*" because no such mark exists. The maximum that one can put on a diploma is "*très bien*," which is what I got. *Maintenant je suis une "cosmète."*

The major event in her career in France, however, was meeting Igor Stravinsky in February 1921. She has often told the story of Serge Diaghilev's inviting her to dinner and saying that Stravinsky would be there and was very moody. Now she reveals the reason for the composer's sulkiness: Chanel had jilted him for the

[1] She underwent an unnecessary appendectomy in Paris in 1934, and an unnecessary thyroid operation in Los Angeles in November 1952.
[2] A letter from Stravinsky's wife Catherine, 31 January 1936, indicates that this work continued into the 1930s: "And how is Vera? Has she given up her flowers or is she still working on them?"

Grand Duke Dmitri.[3] Later in the year, Diaghilev chose the future Mme Stravinsky for the role of Queen in the Ballets Russes revival, in London, of *The Sleeping Beauty*. Although she had been trained at the Nelidova Ballet School in Moscow, she had never aspired to become a ballerina, and after nearly three months in this part she withdrew to devote herself to other interests.

Vera's main work in the 1920s was designing costumes for Diaghilev at her Maison Verâme atelier, where she employed more than a score of midinettes. Her first commission was to design and make the costume for Alicia Markova as the Mechanical Nightingale in the 1925 revival of *Le Chant du Rossignol*. Vera then contributed substantially to the wardrobe of the 1926 Ballets Russes *Firebird*. Recognizing her additional talent for diplomacy, Diaghilev asked her to revise Marie Laurencin's drawings for *Les Biches* and Georges Rouault's for *Le Fils Prodigue* (May 1, 1929), for which Vera also executed the costumes.

Naturally such a woman also made costumes—as distinguished from mere dresses—for herself. "I design my own clothes," she says, "for the reason that I know better than anyone what I have to hide." At present, the sewing for these is done by Erminia Tomici, who comes every Sunday, while shoes, "*en soie*, because I do not like leather," are made during an annual stay in Venice. Many of Mme Stravinsky's robes, as brightly colored as her paintings, never tailored and always feminine, are in empire style, with ribbons, flounces, drapes, puffed sleeves. Her jewelry is large and also self-designed, and she matches her outfits with turbans, headbands, and snoods. As for stockings, not even during New York's arctic winters would she consent to wear *them*.

At 7 a.m. Mme Stravinsky makes her own breakfast, a croissant, or a bagel, and coffee. She then goes to her studio, which used to be her husband's, for two or three hours of painting, and begins work just as he did, by criticizing and making changes in that of the previous day. To a California art teacher who once told her that a painter must first visualize the forms that he plans to represent, she said that *her* method was to "put a spot of color on an empty space and let my fantasy develop the picture." Fantasy is the *sine qua non* of her life. (To those who protest their lack of it, her advice is to become a collector.) "Fantasy is poetry," she says, and she reads Pushkin, Akhmatova, and other Russians almost every day. Though more rarely, she also reads German, French, and English poets, all in the original languages, as well as, in the case of certain poems by Mandelstam and Kuzmin, in the original *manuscripts*, which she preserves in a souvenir album of her years in the Crimea and the Caucasus. Poetry inspires her paintings, and some of them incorporate lines and even whole stanzas from Mayakovsky, Kuzmin, and Lydia Chukovskaya.

Mme Stravinsky believes that her art and her temperament are "romantic," and that the first mark of this is her independence. She has always resented authority, and still avoids navy blue because her governesses were required to wear it. In her Moscow boarding school, she cut study hours to go to the theater, and at her graduation piano recital, she played a radical modern piece by Scriabin. What

[3] Dmitri, with Felix Yussupov, was best-known as one of Rasputin's assassins, an event (December 1916) that earned Stravinsky's gratitude. His friend Lydia Botkina wrote to him from the Pension Beaulite, Sierre, April 6, 1916: "Rasputin's name has been changed to '*Novyi*.' Isn't it awful that the whole of Russia has become the toy of a single man, that he is allowed to go free, supported by our own autocratic system?"

was truly scandalous conduct for a well-bred, well-educated young lady, however, was to work as an actress, and, even worse, to become a cinema star, as she did in 1915. More shocking still, at the beginning of 1913, she abandoned an early, conventional marriage and eloped to Paris with the celebrated artist Serge Sudeikin, exchanging a sheltered, haut-bourgeois life for a bohemian one, among poets, painters, and musicians. Sudeikin was employed by Diaghilev to work on the sets of *Le Sacre du printemps*, but whether or not the young couple were still in Paris at the time of the premiere is not known. Mme Stravinsky's only surviving document from this period is a dinner invitation ("to Vera Arturovna Sudeikina"), March 11, 1913, to the country house—at Volven Bosh, near Antwerp—of Vladimir Ivanovich Gavrilov. Vera and Sudeikin lived in Moscow in 1914 and 1915, though Vera worked in the cinema under the name Mme Shilling, and in St. Petersburg from March 1916 to the spring of 1917, when they fled to the Crimea. There, if not before, Sudeikin discovered her talent as a painter, guided and encouraged her, and helped to organize her first exhibition, in Yalta in 1918.

If Mme Stravinsky's descriptions of her adventures in the Russian Revolution convey the exhilaration but not the dangers of those years, one of the reasons is that she had had almost no experience of fear. "As a child I was frightened only once, from reading the brothers Grimm, after which I had a nightmare. I was afraid, too, going from Yalta to Batum on a small boat in a violent storm, until I lifted the tarpaulin that was protecting me and saw a bright star." Not only was the mast broken, but also, the Sudeikins' lives were rudderless. Nevertheless, the next two years, in Tiflis and Baku, were happy ones. "I learned that poverty stimulates the imagination," Mme Stravinsky asserts, and, whatever the truth of this, she is convinced that "I could lead a simple life again." Yet it is more demonstrably certain that she also enjoys luxuries, though not those associated with the formality, the protocol, and the absence of spontaneity which she deplores in New York social life.

Knowing more about Igor Stravinsky than anyone else, his widow is constantly being asked about him. To the inevitable question concerning his most striking characteristics, she answers, "His logical mind and his originality. 'An artist must follow rules,' he used to say, 'but he must find the rules himself.' If I complained that I had run out of ideas, he would answer that, 'Idleness is a sin: the Muse comes when she sees that you are already making an effort.' He would also say that when he started to compose he was never certain of what he was *going* to do but always certain of what he *wanted* to do. I like the comment about Stravinsky by Liudmilla Pitoëff, who danced the part of the Princess in the first performance of *Histoire du soldat*: 'His curiosity was so great that he animated everyone around him.'" When asked about the "*really* great people" she has known, Mme Stravinsky answers: "I knew only one."

The marriage between the tall, gentle, always calm, soft-voiced, quintessentially feminine Vera, and the small, bony, always anxious, basso-profundo, quintessentially masculine Igor was made in Heaven. When the two did not complement each other in their likes and dislikes, it was only because these were the same: their love of birds and flowers, for example, and of animals and paintings. Every day Vera would make a list of errands and business chores to be accomplished, and every day Stravinsky would write at the top of it: "First you have to kiss me." To those who found it difficult to comprehend how two such different individuals could have such a harmonious marriage, friends would explain that it was not a harmonic but a contrapuntal relationship. If he could be explosive, and would have been happy surrounded by servants, as in pre-emancipated Russia, she was always unruffled, and abhorred the idea of having anyone do anything for her. Although deeper disparities existed, they did not lead to conflict. Thus, while Stravinsky was dogmatic in religious matters, his widow is "religious *à ma façon*; I think to repeat the same prayers bores God." Does she believe in perdition? "No, only in forgiveness."

Vera Stravinsky's ninetieth year was the most productive in her life. She painted some of her best pictures, had highly successful exhibitions of recent works in London, Paris, and Berlin; and published a book, *Fantastic Cities and Other Paintings*.[4] She also worked on the translation of the extensive diaries that she kept during the Russian Revolution. And she received many hommages, of which the least expected was paid to her on June 4, 1978, when the band leading the Puerto Rico day parade paused before her Fifth Avenue window and played the ending of *Firebird*.

Mme Stravinsky attributes her full and fascinating life to her birth on Christmas Day. May her enchanted life continue, for, as Thomas Mann wrote in his journal almost forty years ago, this "thorough-going *Belle Russe* radiates the most likeable of human qualities."

Robert Craft

[4] Godine Press, Boston, April 17, 1979.

9 *May 1952*. Paris.

Excerpts from Interviews, 1912–1963

"The lucidity of Stravinsky's mind has set us free: His combative strength has won for us rights that we can never lose." Erik Satie (*Les Feuilles Libres*, October–November, 1922)

The Petersburg Gazette[1]   October 10, 1912
(The interview took place in St. Petersburg)

Karsavina and Nijinsky are worthy of their profession. But, besides Karsavina, I should mention Nijinskaya, sister of the famous dancer. She has been phenomenally successful since she left the Imperial Theaters. She is extremely talented, a fascinating ballerina, fully the equal of her brother. When she and her brother dance, the others pale by comparison.

I have come to Petersburg for only a few days to see some people. Diaghilev and I, and everyone connected with his company, are resting now, but in November we will start touring again, this time in Germany. I am currently working with the artist N. K. Roerich on a piece entitled *Vesna Sviasschennaya*. Like everything that I write, it is, rather than a ballet, a fantasia in two parts, without a break, like two movements of a symphony. The subject matter comes from an indeterminate ancient era. The first part is called "The Adoration of the Earth," the second "The Sacrifice." The piece will be performed in Paris, in Gabriel Astruc's new theater on the Champs-Elysées. This theater is being decorated by such artists as Maurice Denis and Bourdin: the former has painted the ceilings, the latter has done the sculptural ornamentation. . . .

I do not feel any particular urge to write operas. What interests me is choreographic drama, the only genre in which I see any movement forward . . .

The Petersburg Gazette   February 27, 1913
(The interview took place in London)

To call the librettist and the ballet-master . . . the authors of a work of music drama is senseless. No one would dream of describing *Elektra* as an opera by Hofmannsthal, despite Hofmannsthal's literary fame, and even though the job of an opera librettist is immeasurably more complex than that of a ballet librettist . . . The authors of the libretto of *Petrushka* are Alexander Benois and myself. M. M. Fokine's participation is limited solely to the choreographic realization.

The New York Herald   May 30, 1917
(The interview took place in Morges)

. . . [My] whole heart [is] with the soldiers, the workers, the tillers of the land and the Nationalists, [I have] no use for a fanatic like Lenin [who is] just as dangerous

[1] This and the following excerpt were translated from the Russian by Stephen Heim.

at the moment as Turmer was previously. [I] greatly regret the resignation of M. Miliukov, with whose foreign policy [I was] entirely in agreement, and . . . [his] successor, M. Tereshchenko[2] . . . was an able man in industrial affairs, but as Minister of Foreign Affairs he was an unknown quantity, lacking all training and experience. M. Kerensky [is] a man of great moral strength and intelligence and thoroughly reliable, and about the only one now in power who can restrain the extremists, at present in the minority. . . .

Entries from a Music Sketchbook (c. May 1917)[3]

Music has greater dimensionality than painting (and in this, music is similar to sculpture). Perhaps this explains why the process of its development is slower than the development process in painting.

* * *

The soul of Latins is closer to us Slavs than the soul of Anglo-Saxons, not to mention the Germans, those human caricatures. The Germans are *wunderkind*, but they were never young. The Germans are *Überwunderkind*, since they will never be old either. This is not true of Spain. She is very moving in her old age. And will France really be deprived of the twilight *she* deserves, and deserves more than any other country?

* * *

Constant, unchanging devotion is valueless (not fruitful). Such devotion, it seems to me, is the result of laziness or destructiveness.

Examples: 1) Picasso said he does not like Cézanne.
      2) A number of obscurantists and blockheads like the Swiss composers Doret, Lauber, Sutter and other such riff-raff, have no *respect* for masters.

* * *

I have noticed that those people who talk most about atonality have a very weak understanding of tonality and its systems.

* * *

Sometimes we think that ''taste'' is meaningless, but when you listen to Scriabin, you change your mind.

* * *

People judge music from the perspective of their personal likes and dislikes, as though there were universal agreement as to the truth of the saying ''There's no accounting for taste'' (''*C'est une affaire de goût*''). Then there are others, less naive, who feel that this is a far from adequate basis on which to judge a piece of music, and who try at least to disguise such an attitude. But these more intelligent people can go no further because they lack musical culture.

* * *

[2] Tereshchenko had given his impressions of the Ballets Russes to Aleksandr Blok, who wrote about them in a notebook, March 21, 1913: ''There is something frightening about [Diaghilev], he does not walk alone: art, he says, is a stimulus to sensuality; there are two geniuses: Nijinsky and Stravinsky . . . Everything about Diaghilev is terrible and significant, including his active homosexuality.''
[3] Translated from the Russian by Malcolm Macdonald.

Why is it that changes can take place within me from one year to another, and that these changes are considered legitimate phenomena resulting from man's constant and vital appetite for change—whereas in Art such phenomena are cause for reproach?

Paris-Midi[4]
(The interview was written by G. Suarez)

January 13, 1921

. . . Are you aware that I do not like Wagner? . . . In principle, I refrain from discussing Wagner's work, for its inspiration escapes my modern spirit; furthermore, I do not feel competent to judge the philosophy which too frequently dominates the master of Bayreuth . . . With Wagner, the musical form is enslaved by the text, while the opposite should be true . . . To make the form cohere, he is led into age-old tricks of modulation.

Wagner had an admirable comprehension of the wind instruments and he knew how to use these ensembles with a mastery worthy of the best composers of military fanfares. To attain the sublime, which his pride and vanity required, he mixed the woodwinds and brass with an army of string instruments, thus diverting them from their authentic sonorous purpose. The musician whom I consider to be the greatest in the world, as well as the greatest master of the instrumentation of harmony we have ever had, and I mean Mozart, always avoided that trap, because, a perfect artist, he foresaw the troublesome consequences.

. . . Wagner was a prodigiously gifted musician. . . . Do not say that he was a [genius gone awry.] This leads me to repeat that I entirely share the opinion of Nietzsche, who had the great courage . . . to contrast Bizet, whom I admire infinitely, to the idol of Bayreuth. Moreover, Wagner's Judaic origins clashed too violently with Nietzsche's Slavic affinities for these two geniuses ever to understand each other . . .

Le Matin (Antwerp)
(The interview took place in Antwerp and was written by Guy Davenel)

January 10, 1924

I have always admired [Belgium]. We used to discuss this country at length in school, because the science of counterpoint originated here, and this is as necessary to music as exercise is to the health of the body. I have practiced the science passionately, for it is the architectural base of all music, regulating and guiding all composition. Without counterpoint, melody loses its consistency and rhythm.

Rhythm, to my understanding, becomes music itself. Thus the works of Bach, whom I consider the imperishable model for us all, consist only of rhythm and architecture. The rhythm is an integral and dominant part; but the Romantics make an ornament of it, a flourish. I write my music "in cold blood," and I attempt to incorporate the great ideas that fecundate humanity in each new generation. For this reason, I demand that conductors of my music respect my intentions strictly, injecting their own aesthetic as little as possible. I specify very few nuances. At the moment, I am working on a Concerto for piano and orchestra, which I force myself to play every day without employing the pedals . . . This is so difficult that I am building muscles like Carpentier's—a substitute for physical culture.

[4] The French interviews were translated by Kristin Crawford and Robert Craft.

[I work] an enormous amount, and I am strong. I have an aversion to prolonged repose; for me to sleep more than eight hours is impossible. Automatically, like an alarm, my bounding vitality tears me from the arms of Morpheus, once the dose is fulfilled. . . .

The last work of my venerable master Rimsky-Korsakov was composed before my eyes, in effect, since I was his student at the time. [In Belgium] *Le Coq d'or* has enjoyed the success that it deserves, thanks to the Flemish Opera. I would like to see your theater stage one of my works, *Histoire du soldat* (which is soon to be done in London), a curious and tragic Russian tale which I made in collaboration with [C.-F.] Ramuz, the good Swiss poet. . . .

All my ballets are conceived symphonically, and their initial foundation is almost classical . . . For instance, I have taken three episodes from *Petrushka* and arranged them according to the three traditional movements of the sonata. . . .

Madrid ABC[5]

March 25, 1924

(The interview took place in Madrid)

. . . I like very few modern composers. Manuel Falla is a very eminent musician, cultured and delicate. Then there is my compatriot Prokofiev, whose seductiveness is stunning . . .

In France [I like] Bizet, Gounod, Chabrier, Debussy, and Delibes. I adore *Carmen, Faust, Le Médicin malgré lui*, and *Philémon et Baucis*. In Russia: Tchaikovsky . . . *The Nutcracker, Eugene Onegin, The Queen of Spades*, and sections of the symphonies are of an incomparable rhythmic beauty . . . The critics have not treated Tchaikovsky justly. Their prejudice against him is a result of the admiration that tasteless people have felt for him. Tchaikovsky's music is very easy, for which reason he has been considered vulgar. He is, in reality, the most Russian of Russian composers. I acknowledge the great merits of Mussorgsky and Borodin—the only composers of "The Five" who interest me—but I prefer Tchaikovsky. To make Russian music it is not necessary to speak a barbarous tongue or to wear an oriental caftan . . . I am referring, above all, to Rimsky-Korsakov. I felt true admiration for him when he was my teacher, but now I perceive the artificiality of his Russianism and orientalism . . . To my mind, [Verdi's] best opera is *Rigoletto* . . .

I have very little time for reading, [but in French] I admire the novelist Marcel Proust and the poet Jean Cocteau. Of the young Russian poets, I prefer Essenin and Mayakovsky . . .

At present the *Firebird, Petrushka*, and the *Sacre* interest me less than my new works, such as the Concertino, which is characteristic of my new musical aesthetic. . . .

La Noche[6]

March 25, 1925

(The interview took place in Barcelona and was written by Rafael Moragas)

I am composing a piano sonata . . . finishing it now. I will probably introduce it in Paris next May. Now I am going to Rome. I want to be in Italy. I adore

---

[5] Translated from the Spanish by Kristin Crawford.
[6] Translated from the Spanish by Malcolm Macdonald.

everything Latin, as you know . . . I am working very hard and hope next year to introduce entirely new programs of my music . . .

Excessive glory can be a problem. Let me explain. Recently in Philadelphia I was given tribute by . . . two thousand elderly ladies!! . . . They had me sit on a throne and then proceeded to parade in front of me, each one kissing my hand. When the eight-hundredth one passed, I could not bear any more of it. I excused myself as best I could and told them not to come looking for me because, by the time I got to Europe, my hand would be utterly wasted, and I would not be able to conduct concerts. Worst of all, I had to tell them all of this over a loudspeaker so that they could hear me. . . .

National Tendende[7]   November 25, 1925
(The interview took place in the Palmhaven Restaurant, Copenhagen)

I was here a year and a half ago and conducted an evening in Tivoli Gardens. The people in Copenhagen were so nice to me—I do not think I shall ever forget it . . . But what I like most about Denmark is that it is H. C. Andersen's homeland. He is a poet who has done more to bring nations together than all the politicians put together. He has united mankind regardless of racial or linguistic differences. Whenever I come to Denmark, I dream of being able to read his fairy tales in Danish. Quite possibly the original versions contain a few profound truths, a few thoughts and psychological insights that are lost in translation. . . .

I just came from Frankfurt-am-Main where the younger audience liked my compositions. The sons and daughters cheered, which I naturally love to see, while their parents were wary of me and shook their heads gravely, which I also like to see.

Earlier this year I heard one of my compositions conducted by Mr. Stock in Chicago. It was extraordinary; better, in fact, than I would have done myself. But I did not tell him afterwards when we chatted, because the compliment would have been interpreted as trite, and, besides, he is far too good an artist.

Evening Standard   July 8, 1926
(The interview took place in London on July 8)

I have suffered from critics for many years. They are forever speaking of progress in music, sometimes not differentiating between progress and music . . . Without movement you get stagnation, and it has always seemed to me thát the movement of music is like the rotation of the earth: you know it happens but you do not see it. . . .

Since the time of Tchaikovsky, the relation of ballet and music has changed. Before that master's time, the composer . . . was ordered to write a series of numbers to fit in with the dancing. Now the ballet composer writes a composition to which the dancers must apply their art. It is their work to fit in their dances . . .

I am not a revolutionary in anything, least of all in music. Mothers are always a little apprehensive of children who want to run too fast. I am one of those children, but my critics call me revolutionary.

[7] The Scandinavian and Hungarian interviews were translated by Berlitz.

March 25, 1928

. . . We talk about the intellectual and spiritual good which St. Thomas Aquinas embodied . . . Stravinsky is deeply interested in the great mystics; we ask him about Saint John of the Cross, about Saint Teresa. At the mention of Teresa of the Perfect Jesus, Stravinsky's eyes suddenly light up with admiration . . . He comments on various saints—Jerome, for one—and religious philosophers—Soloviev, among others—and we discuss Ramon Llull at length; Stravinsky is deeply interested in our great mystic.

In *Oedipus Rex*, Stravinsky attributes much significance to the way in which the relationship between word and music is to be understood. He talks at length about his earlier experiment in this regard in *Les Noces*. His eagerness to purify music of extra-musical elements is well-known, and he is no less eager to purge words of extra-musical content. Objections have been voiced: "Why does he introduce words into his music at all?" The explanation is that he does not want to deprive himself of that wonderful instrument, the human voice . . . But he is more interested in employing words for their purely musical potential than for their psychological expressiveness and dramatic significance. He tells us that in *Oedipus* the word is musically functional material, in the way that marble and stone are the sculptor's material. Thus *Noces* contains verse songs, but the Russian words do not combine to make logical sense; instead, they are arranged strictly according to their sonorous and rhythmic potential. *Oedipus* represents a much more advanced step in this experiment. An active language, Stravinsky tells us, will always contain elements of emotional and sentimental evocation, no matter how hard the composer tries to eliminate them, and these detract from the musical value of the word. For this reason, Stravinsky has reverted to a dead language . . . and because it is known universally through its diffusion by the Church and is therefore no shock to the ear, as Sanskrit and Greek might be . . . Stravinsky has kept the Latin meter intact; and he has made little games of musical values established in syllables, feet, shorts, and longs, etc. . . . . The choice of the Oedipus myth was also dictated by the principle of alienating the audience from all dramatic and extra-musical interest: for this purpose, Stravinsky chose a story known throughout the world. Precisely this concept of word-material-music has alienated Stravinsky from the song, or the "*Lied*," which he cultivated so gloriously in younger years.

The magnificent proof of Stravinsky's musical purification is the *Sacre*: the absence of dance makes it richer, not poorer, because the audience is not distracted from the formal qualities of the work . . . its architectonic severity, its extreme purity of form and line, its marvelous conceptual clarity . . . After the dress rehearsal of *Petrushka*, we ask Stravinsky: "If this work is not considered classical, I do not know what the word means . . . Classical in the good sense, of course . . ."

[8] Translated from the Catalonian by Malcolm Macdonald.
[9] Though most of Señor Mayoral's article quotes Stravinsky only indirectly, the interview has been included because it contains unique statements about *Oedipus* and *Apollo* before the latter had been performed in Europe and before the former was published or known in Spain.

I.S.: "The word classical always has a good connotation."

M.: "But classicism often means formula, the academic, the servile imitation of the old."

I.S.: "True, but who is responsible for these confusions?"

M.: "Do you enjoy being a classicist?"

I.S.: "The qualification honors me."

M.: "Are you pleased to be called 'modern'?"

I.S.: "No, never that! . . . The modernist, the avant-garde, everything that seeks to limit to a trend is repugnant to me. The era of 'isms' and manifestos ended fifteen years ago. Now you find these things only in the provinces."

Stravinsky talks with us about *Apollon Musagète*. The protagonist is Apollo himself, wearing a crown of laurel. The concept of the ballet is very simple, and the dances, which include the "Pas de Deux," are classical. The set design will portray the classical forest, palms, a temple. The first scene represents Apollo's birth . . . A chorus of goddesses hails the infant from Olympus. In the second scene, he is entrusted to three of the muses, Calliope, Polyhymnia and Terpsichore, and, later still, to mortals . . . A tone of slight mockery, in the manner of Leucon, is noticeable throughout. Stravinsky tells us that the music is a very simple composition of lines and combinations. One perhaps surprising detail is that Stravinsky has put verses in the mouths of his characters, verses by Boileau— "a great and marvelous poet," the composer says, the verses "come from the work naturally most blasphemed by anarchists and romantics, *L'Art Poétique*."

Le Journal de Genève
November 14, 1928

. . . It is not possible to create in the language of a past generation. Furthermore, the old masters had something to say, unlike the champions of "the good old days," who want, not art, but routine. . . .

It would be difficult for me to say who has done me more harm, my followers or my detractors. As soon as one does something new, a pirate appropriates it for himself, while friends and imitators water it down, to make it clearer and easier to understand. True, people welcome the new more readily in diluted form. But when they drink this watery substance and do not discover the taste of wine, they do not blame those who added water to the wine but find fault with the quality of the wine itself. . . .

*   *   *

How many times have I been told that my music is too geometrical! Order and geometry! But the essence of art, the meaning of creative work, is to give definite form to that which was amorphous . . .

Les Nouvelles Littéraires
December 8, 1928

(The interview was written by Florent Fels)

. . . My first idea for *Petrushka* was to make a "*Konzertstück*," a kind of combat between the piano and the orchestra. That idea was incorporated . . . in the second scene, Petrushka's Cell. My first conception was of a man with long hair wearing white tie and tails: the romantic stereotype of the musician or poet. I conceived of him sitting at the piano and rolling bizarre objects on the keyboard, while the orchestra protested vehemently, in sonorous punches. This is not a fable;

the attraction for me was not folkloric . . . [Folklore] is a delectation, and that is not my aim. Petrushka is not a symbol but a living being; his picturesque quality and his transformation were not what interested me. This is a carnival tale, the dramatic equivalent of my first idea, in which Petrushka, Pierrot, the pianist, the musician, the poet, becomes entangled in the most banal intrigue, the most deliberately banal intrigue in the world.

The Charlatan is the pivot, the matter-of-fact being who reveals that Petrushka is full of song. Oblivious to the song in his heart and his whimsical spirit, [the Charlatan] makes Petrushka into a commercial object. That is sometimes called symbolic. Let us call it *truth*, because the poet never dies.

I composed *Firebird* during the winter of 1909–10. I wrote *Petrushka* in Beaulieu-sur-mer and Rome during the winter of 1910–11. The idea for the dramatic action resulted from the fact that I did not want to call my first attempt ''*Konzertstück*.'' When the name ''Petrushka'' came to me, I saw that a story would flow easily from all the romantic . . . elements implicit in such a name.

My original conception corresponds to the second act. In order to live, Petrushka needed a setting, and a love, and thus I created the four-part burlesque scene which was just recorded.

A month ago I came to Paris to record *Firebird*. This was my second recording experience; that of *Petrushka* in London was my first. Nothing could be more strenuous. Striving for the best possible performance, one must repeat the piece endlessly; one's weariness accumulates, and when nerves are about to snap, the violinists' arms to succumb, and the mind to go blank with the monotony of the task, that is the moment when one must be perfect for the ''take'' which is to be recorded. Never have I known such exertion. The idea of being my own critic, listening coldly to myself in front of an apparatus, without taking part in the orchestral action, powerless to correct any weakness, any mechanical defect, makes even the most cruel of criticisms pale by comparison.

Imagine, moreover, that after one satisfactory trial performance, the piece is repeated three more times, and the final recording will be chosen from one of these last.

On the phonograph, the exact tone is obtained by the speed with which the work is performed. Thus I had to gain three seconds in a 3 minute 55 second segment and start the recording of this fragment over again three times in succession at the same speed, regulated by the chronometer, like a contest in the Olympics.

From my experience with recording, I have learned that while the phonograph is not yet classed as a new instrument, it could easily become one, if a composer were to write specifically for it, for its timbre, as I did for the mechanical piano.

The extraordinary velocity of the phono offers a new musical substance. If music requires reproduction and not reading (since the ear, not the visual intellect, is the judge), one could say that the phono gives an image of an image, rather than a transformation. I think that in future recordings, the aim will not be to reproduce a piano, a violin, an orchestra; the phono will be an end in itself, an absolute instrument, offering a constant melodic timbre, a particular sound and a pure tone.

When I played my works on the mechanical piano, I transmitted, through the intermediary of electricity, sounds which in no way corresponded to my immediate sentiments, because I had an interpreter. For that reason I explained to

Erik Satie that I sought, in the mechanical piano, an instrument destined not to reproduce my works, but to recreate them.

I insisted on conducting the Columbia recordings of *Firebird* and *Petrushka* myself, because, by this perhaps not yet sufficient but already gratifying means, I endeavored to engrave my traditions, my will, and to show in what spirit I wish my works to be performed. If a discrepancy exists between my podium and microphone performances, I still find a greater veracity in that than when the baton is entrusted to a[nother] conductor, no matter how intelligent or respectful he might be of my work.

Thus the phonograph is currently the best instrument through which the masters of modern music can transmit their thoughts.

Neue Badische Landes-Zeitung[10]   December 8, 1930[11]
(The interview took place in Mannheim and was written by Karl Laux)

Tempo is the basic problem of conducting, much more than "poeticizing." A creative aspect exists in the treatment of tempo, in that one "creates" a given object, namely, tempo . . .

A change of pulse-rate cannot be imposed upon a human being without endangering him; similarly, the tempo in music must be treated with utmost care. Tempo is more than a means, just as the word is more than a means: the word has a magic import and creative strength, and so evolves from a means to an end. Life is inherent in tempo, too; it is an organism. The proof of this is found in the rhythm of a march, which varies from nation to nation. These variations are not deliberate or calculated but natural, corresponding to the physical properties of that people, their walking stride. . . .

Modern music does not exist. Music is not a matter of fashion. New music does exist, at least inasmuch as we speak a different language today from those that people spoke in the past. What we say is the same as what was said before; only the expression has changed. Goethe explains this . . .

In *Le Baiser de la fée* . . . I discovered a new Tchaikovsky. While the famous [Russian] "Five" turned consciously to the old-Russian picturesque music, making it an exportable item, a kind of bazaar, the Russian element in Tchaikovsky (as also in Glinka) is quite naive. Tchaikovsky's music mixes a Russian colloquial and a European idiom, but Tchaikovsky did not transform his works into "Russian music." He is a great master of pure music, whereas in symphonic form the Germans (for example, Brahms) are more valuable. In Tchaikovsky, [I] particularly value the rhythmic quality, so abundant in the few works of his that are performed regularly . . . and I always defend [Tchaikovsky] against his most popular works. By composing in the memory of Tchaikovsky [I intend] to make a portrait with him as [my] model— just as a painter creates something new from his model (which is what distinguishes a portrait from a photograph), so the musician portrays a new Tchaikovsky but preserves his features . . .

[10] The translations from the German are by Helen Reeve.
[11] Stravinsky conducted a concert with the Philharmonischer Verein in Mannheim on December 9, 1930.

(The interview took place in Trieste and was written by Vittorio Tranquilli)

I have mastered myself through the evolution of my spirit. By following the precepts laid down in the Gospels, I have sought to realize the man inside me. . . .

It cannot be asserted that one art or art form is born primarily of [intrinsic] sentiment, while another is visually inspired, born [strictly] of the eyes. The artist, the musician, acts and creates under the influence of all five senses. . . .

The romantic of the past century (and the belated romantics of this century) expresses [only] his individual sentiment. Individualism, which dominated all art in the past, still prevails in the romantic. He explores [only] his [innate], individual universe, selecting subjects according to [sentimental] inspiration. Today we are in an anti-romantic and anti-individualistic period.

Art is not purely subjective but has become objective, drawing elements from the outside, the external [as well as from internal sentiment]. For many years, we have been victims of the individualist invasion. Sentiment has been exaggerated in art, taken to the extreme, to the point of exhaustion. In reaction, and, if I am not mistaken, for natural reasons, contemporary art is anti-individualist; but this does not necessarily preclude personality [as distinct from individuality].

Personality can be operative in a work of art while at the same time remaining detached from individual sentiment. The existence of personality does not obstruct a larger perspective: man's particular feeling can be contemplated by a personality, but so, too, can the position of man in the universe [whereas the individualist perspective is self-obsessed and narrow]. This more universal view provides the artist with a more solid base, and . . . the life of his creation attains a higher and more significant function.

Individualism in art, philosophy, and religion implies a state of revolt against God. Look at Nietzsche's antiChrist. The principle of individualism, and of atheism, is contrary to the principle of personality and subordination before God: in the former we find the superman, in the latter we recognize men.

I am a traditional musician, neither revolutionary nor conservative, and my traditionalism has a definite parentage. Art cannot go backwards; the wall of history behind us is insurmountable. In music as in biology, the father exists in the son, and, genealogically, I am a product of all of the old masters whom I admire. If I remake Pergolesi's music, I do so not to repeat it or to correct it, but simply because I feel myself to be a brother in spirit to the composer, and because I need to invoke his musical spirit to become prolific and fecund. This phenomenon is called love. It is love, the union of two spirits, that draws me to Pergolesi . . .

I hear and see music. All my senses, and in fact my total physical being, participate in the act of musical creation. But the principal element and determining factor in the composer's work is hearing. If my ear is not pleased, my creative instinct does not respond. The ear has its own appetite, and it assembles, assimilates, orders and elaborates the construction, as the mouth does food . . . The ear is the mouth of music. But I use the word "appetite" in the spiritual sense, as St. Augustine uses it in describing the appetite of the soul, which both exalts and sublimates itself as it gains more appetite for Light and for God. Both the imaginative faculty and our musical ear are sterile without light, grace, and

[12] The translations from the Italian are by Kristin Crawford and Robert Craft.

guidance from above. To be worthy to receive these we must pray in the purest manner and strip the soul of its inferior appetites.

Münchner Telegramm Zeitung und Sport-Telegraf
(The interview took place in Munich)

February 2, 1933

Unfortunately, I must continually emphasize that I am in no sense a revolutionary, either in my general views or in my art, and I was never a Communist, materialist, atheist, or Bolshevik, as is frequently said of me . . . Many people cannot understand that I am simply a man of our times and an artist of our times; and I believe that I have grasped the special character of this time in art. Of course, I always assume a certain musical content . . . Too often, alas, and even in such a musically educated and trained country as Germany, one encounters only conventional values and sensibilities. People say: this is not a good work . . . Their reaction is as if someone who happened not to like raspberries (I like them) were to say: raspberries are an impossibility, without recognizing the subjective nature of such a conclusion. People must keep in mind that a contemporary artist cannot adopt a traditional style, that I cannot compose in the style of Brahms or Schumann, whom I value highly. I believe that we have unique, contemporary tasks, as did the composers in the seventeenth-century tongue. Evidently people find all of this abstruse. The audience always wants to be accustomed to something first. Beethoven is understood now, or is believed to be understood, and people know Bach—therefore, they are accepted. People nowadays feel comfortable pitting the great masters of the past against a musician of today, against a "cultural Bolshevik." Well, perhaps in 25 years people will hold up my works, with which they will have become comfortable, as examples of real music to the then younger composers.

Corriere della Sera
(The interview took place on February 9 in the lounge of Stravinsky's hotel in Milan)

February 10, 1933

I have crossed the Alps almost every year since 1911, when I finished *Petrushka* in Rome, and the first piano rehearsals for the ballet took place there. To play or conduct in one of your concert halls or theaters—my first time was in Rome with Diaghilev—has always given me the greatest joy.

I do not have different styles. I simply follow my road. When I am asked to define my position, to categorize, anatomize, I shudder.

[Interviewer: You are recognized as the leader of modern music.]

Perhaps. But there are good and bad modern musicians. I am Stravinsky and that is enough.

Verdi pleases me enormously, much more than Wagner.[13] Verdi's music translates feelings and passions, it is vivid and animated, it is theatrical, and it is

[13] One of the Russian newspapers in Paris published an article for Stravinsky's fiftieth birthday, June 18, 1932, an unsigned piece but written by someone who clearly knew him in 1907–08. This anonymous author writes that "At a time when everyone was praising Wagner's aesthetics, Stravinsky said that they were of no consequence to him. He called Verdi 'A titan of dramatic music.'" The article repeats the anecdote that when Stravinsky showed the score of a part of *Fireworks* to Rimsky-Korsakov, the latter remarked, "You have a great talent, but one can compose such music only when one reaches my age." Stravinsky sarcastically wrote "Splendid" in the margin next to this and at the head of the article, "What idiot wrote this?"

beautiful music in itself . . . I began to compose when Tchaikovsky died, and my nostalgia for his music is profound and lifelong. I dedicated *Le Baiser de la fée* to Tchaikovsky's muse . . . Debussy is still too close to me, too much alive in me, in us, for me to speak of him with detachment.[14] I still hear his voice, his works still echo in my ears, and if I close my eyes, I see him before me. One of the last times that we were together, we talked about Puccini.[15] Debussy had a genuine esteem for Puccini and knew and liked many pages of his music. I had a friendly feeling for him, too, and he invited me to Torre del Lago. Alas, he died before I could go.

Pesti Hirlap[16]
(The interview was written by Fothy János)

My next work will be stage music, neither opera, nor ballet, but rather, if you insist on a label, melodrama. A Greek mystery play, the story of *Perséphone*, as told by Homer . . . There will be a soloist: the priest. The other singers are a chorus and a children's choir. The premiere will take place in Paris in December. *Perséphone* is my fourth composition inspired by a Greek or Roman subject, following *Oedipus Rex*, *Apollon Musagète*, and *Duo concertant*. This last work was created under the influence of Virgil's pastoral idylls.[17]

If you perceive in me the proponent of a new classicism, then you misunderstand. My art is aiming in a canonical direction; for me, all great and pure art must be canonical or ecclesiastical in spirit, the spirit built on the concept of recognition through knowledge. I want the audience not just to hear the music, but also to recognize and know it. To hear and to comprehend are not the same. It is easy to hear and at the same time recognize the works of the old masters on the basis of familiarity and habit. Today's music must be listened to in such a way that passive hearing extends to active recognition and knowledge. In other words, the hearing must be free of all that is familiar, habitual, inherited . . . Whoever wishes to follow my intentions will be able to do so, and whoever can do that can also understand me. . . .

[14] In a letter to Willy Strecker on March 9, 1932, Stravinsky thanks the publisher "for the Debussy pieces . . . a very beautiful edition."

[15] In June 1922, Puccini wrote from Viareggio to a lady in Ruegen: ". . . I think that if Stravinsky wishes, the sun of Puccini has gone down. Yet the royalties do not decrease, which means that the world still enjoys my sunset. *Turandot* is a subject that would seem to require a morbid treatment, but I remain normal with modern intentions . . ."

[16] This and the following three interviews were published in Budapest newspapers on March 29–31, 1933. The press conference apparently took place on March 28, and Stravinsky probably spoke German, since one of the accounts, not included here, is in that language. But whatever the linguistic barrier, the discrepancies in quoting the composer are insignificant compared to the astonishing degree of agreement. Stravinsky had been invited to Budapest to conduct a "Composers' Soirée" in which his Concerto was played by a 14-year-old prodigy from Chicago, Rosalinda Kaplan. The concert took place on April 3, and Stravinsky stayed in the Carlton Hotel March 27–April 4.

[17] Some of the program notes for the *Duo concertant* used in Stravinsky's British tour, February 22–28, 1934 (Manchester, Liverpool, Cambridge, London, Oxford) were signed "I.S." and some "Edwin Evans," though the latter's information came from Stravinsky. The direct quote from "I.S." concludes ". . . for many years I had taken no pleasure in the blend of strings, struck in the piano, with strings, set in vibration by the bow. In order to reconcile myself to this instrumental combination, I was compelled to turn to the minimum of instruments . . . only two . . . Thus originated the idea of the Duo concertant for violin and piano. The mating of these instruments seems much clearer than the combination of a piano and several stringed instruments which tends to confusion with the orchestra." Evans's description of the first part of the "Cantilène" as a "perpetuum mobile," and his comment that the beginning of "Eclogue I suggests a *loure* or Musette," are clearly Stravinsky's.

Magyarsag

Creativity can endure if it is necessary and natural. Precisely because of this, we cannot talk of progress; trees grew 2,000 years ago exactly as they do now. Whatever I do, I find natural, and I always know what I must do; this is the essence of creation, to select the material and then purify it. Only if we are in control of what we wish to express can we proceed to work—though of course this does not happen suddenly . . . Usually one problem occupies my mind, and I build my work around it. Often I start with technical problems, together with spiritual and philosophical ones, which reinforce or develop one another. Frequently a certain grouping of instruments catches my attention, and I imagine that I will try to create something with a defined instrumental combination. But I am never in a hurry. I have time; my thoughts are maturing in me, and only when I feel the time is right do I start to work. This logic restrains me from working until the technical solution and the creative idea are in a hundred percent correlation. I do not want to give an opinion of my music, and I cannot comment on work-in-progress. Also, I do not like to think back on finished compositions. . . .

One cannot say anything about progress in music,[18] just as, standing at the foot of the mountain, one cannot comment on the panorama as seen from the summit. Each stratum of the audience is different and has its own opinion; to create a work of art that will be understood equally and appeal equally at every level is therefore impossible . . . Even the most cultured public does not accept groundbreaking works. At best, it measures music according to opinions formed a century ago. Rather than develop its own evaluation of the new work, the audience continues with the inherited understanding and customary listening habits, expecting that which is already familiar . . . For this reason, no new music of lasting value has ever been understood in its own time.

The radio has been a tremendous influence, beneficial in the sense that it quickly disseminates [new music] and speeds up the process of understanding . . . But in our technological era, individual activity plays an ever-diminishing part in our lives; the spirit degenerates and art atrophies. Despite the comforts that technology provides, the composer must do his spiritual and intellectual exercises . . . The creative artist will never overthrow older art, but instead he must continually strive to develop it.

This is my third visit to Budapest. I came with Diaghilev and the Russian Ballet before the war, and I was here again in 1926 . . . Among Hungarian composers, I know the works of Béla Bartók[19] and greatly admire them.

UJSAG

(The interview was written by Nagy Endre)

Duo concertant? The title sounds strange only when you first hear it, but just as we talk of quintets, quartets, and trios, so we may speak of duos. I chose the title because I wanted to emphasize that the piano and violin are instruments of equal stature in the composition. "Concertant," however, really means to compete. Thus

---

[18] Another Budapest reporter, Ottlik Palma, quotes Stravinsky: "There is no progress, only evolution and evolution cannot be measured until it is complete."
[19] In another interview, Stravinsky says, "Béla Bartók is a personal friend of mine."

I also indicate with this word that the piano and violin are in competition with each other.[20]

The largest part of the audience listens to the music but does not hear it, even though in most Indo-Germanic languages the verbs "to hear" and "to understand" are related. From this departure point one can speak of passive and active listening. Active audiences actually follow the act of composing when they hear a new musical style, while passive audiences can enjoy only familiar melodies, familiar harmonies, familiar rhythms. This does not mean that music which is not understood by this type of audience *lacks* melody, harmony, and rhythm. Gounod and Bizet were as incomprehensible to the audience of their time as most modern music is for part of today's audience. Today we can hardly comprehend how an audience could have felt that *Carmen* lacks melody, but when the melodies were new, they too required "active listening" . . . A segment of all audiences does not endeavor to nap in its orchestra seats. . . .

What is detrimental about radio is that it renders music familiar, which is not the same as understood . . . Radio discourages real listening, primarily because only he who plays an instrument and experiences the composer's struggles and solutions can understand. Those who do not play an instrument can have only amateur opinions about new music, regardless of how many concerts they attend, staying *until the bitter end*, and regardless of how many thick tomes on the aesthetics of music they have read.

The Manchester Guardian   February 22, 1934
(The interview took place in Manchester, February 21, 1934)[21]

Music is the mother of my music; I am loyal not to the machines but to the old aristocracy of my predecessors. You look surprised. That is because you have heard so many things said of me that are misjudgments.

The American reporters, tumbling aboard my ship when I went for the first time there, said to me: "What do you, the arch-priest of modern music, think of the future?" and I said, "You must go elsewhere. I am no exponent of modernism. How am I to know? This is the present. It is not possible for us to be objective and say, 'This is such-and-such an age.'" It reminds me of an operetta I saw in Paris, set in medieval times, in which a number of knights sing together: "*Nous sommes les chevaliers du moyen âge.*" How do they know?

I do not think it just to give an age a label, and call it "the age of steel" or "the age of noise," for there are so many other manifestations of the age, at least equally appropriate. If you are going to give it a handle, why not "the age of social unrest," or something like that? Simply because a child is unlike its parent, you do not doubt who was its mother, but if a painting or a piece of sculpture or a

[20] Here the interviewer remarks on Stravinsky's addiction to lexical references, and observes that "the artist in exile manifests a special interest in foreign languages, a foreign language complex, the psychoanalysts say. Stravinsky tells us how an archaic French word meaning 'ham' was transformed into the German word '*Geige.*' When Stravinsky talks about criticism, he again begins with references to grammar."
[21] "In Liverpool two days later, en route to a luncheon in his honour by the Sandon Studios, Stravinsky was informed of the death of Elgar. Stravinsky paid a very warm tribute to Elgar, asking the guests to stand for a moment in silence as a mark of respect to him. Stravinsky said he knew many of Elgar's works and attended concerts at which he had conducted. Stravinsky had heard Elgar's *Cockaigne Overture* in St. Petersburg" (*Liverpool Post*, February 24).

symphony is not recognizable at first sight, everybody seems to doubt its organic relationship with the paintings and statues and symphonies that have preceded it.

An artist needs to make use of what he finds ready at hand—the lunging of a piston, the thud of a hammer, the scrape of a chair. But these things are only part of the age and they may or may not be the really significant part. That we shall never know. Only our descendants will be able to tell that. And whatever we use for artistic purposes, we must not fail to see that it is related to the whole, that it has a logic, like literature, for instance.

The concert hall can become too much a habit, and a soporific habit. People go there and listen to the same pieces again and again. I want music to be fresh and alive in the ears of the people. Music ought to be like an opened window that lets in clean air, perhaps cold air, to make the head spin. Music should be desire, not habit . . .

The dance is as old and as young as man. It did not die with the Russian Ballet. It is an essential, a dramatic part of the life of the theater. But there is not a great deal of good ballet music. Either it is sunk in the dance or is irrelevant to it. Music and dance should be a true marriage of separate arts, a partnership, not a dictatorship of the one over the other. Ballet music should have an independent existence. Too often it is tied to the theatrical spectacle.

I believe that music has a most important part to play in the art of cinema, which is a separate art form, only the cinema does not yet recognize the fact. Just as drama plus music made opera, so film plus music will make—what? I do not know, but I feel sure it will be something vital to us, something new.

Il Piccolo [Rome]   May 27, 1935
(The interview took place in Rome)

Here I have discovered my [idea of] heaven. Since we are Russian, Northerners, it is curious that we should feel so at home in Italy, and especially in Rome . . . Russian music and architecture, in other periods, have been deeply influenced by Italian artists . . . How many times have I been in Rome? Very many, perhaps twenty-four or twenty-five. I cannot say exactly. I have many dear friends here. Maestro Molinari,[22] for example. Rome calls to me with her great voice, and I am happy to return, for which reason I am willing to put off my urgent work for at least a week . . .

I am working on the second volume of my autobiography, *Chroniques de ma vie*. The first volume came out a few months ago. I have looked for it in bookstores here in Rome but have not seen it. Soon there will be an Italian translation, done by a Milan publisher. [In Volume I] I spoke about my work through 1920, and now I describe the subsequent period. . . .

[I am also composing a concerto], not for orchestra but for two pianos. The word "concerto" brings to mind a struggle. The piano struggles against the orchestra, the violin against the orchestra. Their strengths are unequal . . .

I regret not being able to present my most recent work, *Perséphone*, on which I spent a year of my life. It was performed in London with Ida Rubinstein, on the occasion of the marriage of the Duke of Kent . . . I prefer the music to be given in

[22] Bernardino Molinari (1880–1952), Italian conductor.

concert form. The staging requires the participation of too many people (scenographers, stage directors, choreographers), as well as endless discussions which shift the focus of attention and entangle the idea . . .

Aftenposten   September 27, 1935

(The interview took place in the Ostbanen Railroad Station, Oslo)

I have written a remarkable duo-piano composition which I shall present in Paris in November . . . Incidentally, this piece is not quite finished, but I have completed a sonata for piano and violin, inspired by Virgil—a strenuous piece, since it is to some extent athematic.

As for my arrangements from *Petrushka* and *Firebird*, the old masters did the same with paintings and etchings, and Liszt transcribed in this way.

Göteborgs Morgonpost   October 11, 1935

I am occasionally asked the question [which contemporary composers I like best], but I never dare to reply. In the first place, it would certainly be unpleasant for the composers to read what I say about them! In the second place, I only talk about things that I enjoy!

Copenhagen Politiken   October 14, 1935

"Understanding" in the general sense has no bearing on music, for music is not composed with understanding, nor is it meant to be understood; a person must have an instinct to grasp music. Also, people loathe innovation . . . Anyone who attempts to break with tradition, compelled by some inner necessity, is compared to the soldier who destroyed Archimedes' circles. What one can safely say is that the crowd will never comprehend genius, or that if the crowd recognizes genius, it is not genius but something else.

Music is much more complex than other art forms, not merely because it employs a new language . . . but because an alien factor exists between the work and the audience, the interpreter, who may or may not completely misunderstand the music himself. One might say that the interpreter's option to understand or misunderstand has been exploited to the utmost. The painting of an artist at least hangs securely on the wall . . . But God help composers . . .

The survival of art depends on a certain sense of well-being, a certain atmosphere of undefined tranquility and edification. But if humanity is gripped by fear, thinking constantly of war, living every hour in distress, time will hardly remain to consider the values expressed by art . . .

A person is constantly changing, and, if he does not atrophy but remains active, the changes are generally for the better . . . The only thing that does not change is stupidity. The devil remains constant; God is forever changing.

A conclusion that costs nothing is worthless; we should pay for everything that we get. We can derive greater benefit by sitting down attentively, alone, and experiencing in person a single composition at the piano than by tuning in to all of the daily broadcasts. Radio has glutted us to the point that we now cannot taste what we are eating.

Radio-Cité, Voix de Paris   November 19, 1935

(The interview was written by Soulima Stravinsky)

. . . The diffusion of music by . . . recordings[23] is a formidable scientific conquest
. . . [that] also presents a great danger, due to the terrible facility with which
anyone anywhere can hear everything without the slightest effort. The vice of
progress lies precisely in this absence of effort, especially in music, which can be
comprehended only by those who approach it through active effort. We are more
conscious of music when we play it ourselves, even if imperfectly. I wonder if the
advantages of propagating music mechanically sufficiently outweigh the
disadvantages . . .

Music is the cause of the most serious misunderstandings, because people want
to look for something in it other than music itself. But it is important to know what
purely sonorous musical concepts exist, independent of what they may readily
suggest, while it is not important to know what the author had in mind while
composing.

Radiodiffusion [Paris]   June 2, 1938[24]

My primary concern when I compose for the theater is to guarantee that the
music has an autonomous existence and does not risk becoming subservient to the
other theatrical elements. To my understanding, the relationship between these
elements and music should be parallel, and in listening to old operas, I am never
shocked by the supposed discord between the form of the musical pieces—arias,
duos, ensembles—and the exigencies of the dramatic action. If I did not conform
entirely to this principle myself in the earliest theatrical works, such as *Firebird*, I
soon felt an imperative need to follow this rule; already in *Petrushka* the
symphonic principle prevails. As for my most recent works, they are conceived
and constructed as musical wholes, independent from their scenic destination. That
is why I urge that they be executed in concert as well as in dramatic form . . .

Radiodiffusion [Paris]   December 24, 1938[25]

. . . There are two brands of *pompier*, the avant-garde and the old-fashioned.
Those who ride the avant-garde bandwagon speak in involved terms, promulgate

[23] Stravinsky had made many recordings at about the time of this interview, including, two weeks
before it, that of the Violin Concerto. *Il Disco*, Milan, September 1934, published an interview with
him, by Domenico de' Paoli, dating from the *Noces* recording session in London in July 1934. Here
the composer says, in part: "The whole work was recorded, and I am satisfied with the results; but
what an unbearably difficult task and what a quantity of minute technical problems have to be
resolved in order to make a good phonic rendition. I happened to have had superb performers—
above all, the chorus, which was British, and sang in English . . . I recorded my Serenade for piano
and the Piano-Rag Music before leaving for London. That was the first time I have played piano
[solos] for a microphone, but I cannot say . . . that I found it more inspiring than an audience. The
Serenade was designed for recording, each of its four parts lasting exactly four minutes—or one side
of a record. The Piano-Rag Music is an eminently phonogenic composition, and the results were
optimum . . ."
[24] The interviewer was Georges Auric, but Stravinsky wrote both the questions and the answers and
read from a typescript. Most of the talk is devoted to the *Dumbarton Oaks* Concerto, and to plans for
an American tour at the beginning of 1939, followed by an Australian tour. He also alludes to "a large
work-in-progress" (the Symphony in C).
[25] The interviewer was Serge Moreux, music critic of *L'Intransigeant*, but Stravinsky had written his
replies beforehand and he read them from a typescript.

music and Freud, music and Marx, and only grudgingly allow themselves to be won over, even by Saint Thomas himself. The simple brand of bandwagoner, in contrast, speaks of music and melody, is utterly consumed in the contemplation of music, loves the sentimental and the oriental picturesque, and holds everything noble in high regard. I have my *Firebird* in mind, but this is not what makes me prefer the latter brand to the former; I simply find the latter less dangerous. In effect, a *pompier* is a *pompier*, and he never succeeds in disguising himself, even when well aware of this in himself. Moreover, I warn those gentlemen who tout the avant-garde: do not be too scornful of your poor old-fashioned colleagues, but fear instead that you will pass out of vogue faster than they do, for the times threaten you more . . .

The crisis is not limited to the arts . . . The entire human condition is profoundly affected: we are losing sight of values, and our sense of proportion is failing us, leading us to violate the fundamental laws of human equilibrium. The effect is two-fold: on the one hand, the character of what I will call high musical mathematics is vitiated, given servile applications, vulgarized by utilitarianism. On the other hand, since the mind of our era is itself diseased, music which is considered pure inherently carries the germs of a pathology resembling a new original sin . . .

The old original sin is essentially a sin of recognition. The new original sin is essentially one of non-recognition, a failure to acknowledge the truth and the laws that flow from it, laws that we have deemed fundamental. What is this truth, in music, and what repercussions does it have on creative activity? We must remember that "the spirit listeth where it will."[26] The key word is will: since the spirit is endowed with the capacity to will. This principle of speculative will is of such an order that to judge it, or even discuss it, is manifestly useless. Music, in its pure form, is free speculation; its creators have always borne testimony to that concept. Personally, I see no reason not to do as they have done. A creature myself, I cannot help having a desire to create, and I cannot keep myself from externalizing that desire. But in order to externalize, one must also possess the means, which are techniques, or simply *technique*, in the most literal sense of the word. The desire to create postulates the technique, which is more significant than is generally supposed. Furthermore, such despised notions as *technique*, *métier*, *artisan* are in urgent need of reclassification. These are realities, and I place them in direct opposition to the nebulous nomenclature of *inspiration*, *art*, *artist*. Hazy terms of this sort impede our perception in a domain that is calculated and balanced, and through which the current of the speculative spirit passes. Only then does the current of speculation arouse emotion, the emotion alleged to be the principle of all creation, and which people like to discuss so impudently, attributing to it a shocking sense which compromises even the thing itself. What value does *emotion* assume if directly derived from speculation?

I am accustomed to contrast personality and individuality. Though often confused, these concepts are in opposition. Individuality is presumptuous, personality self-effacing; the latter subordinates itself, while the former delights in self-infatuation, complacency and rebellion. I bend to the order of created things, an order which I accept and to which I myself belong. My work imposes hierarchies upon me and demands that I submit it to disciplines, and in yielding to these I do not feel that I am going astray.

---

[26] "*Spiritus ubi vult spirat*" (St. John, 3:8).

The most important discipline, though this may seem paradoxical, is taste. Generally, taste is thought to be a privilege of the individual who believes himself free and independent. No: taste is a privilege of personality alone, a natural means of recognizing values, one that must be continually cultivated and vivified, one whose perfectibility springs from the principle of submission, and enlightened, reasoned, voluntary submission.

In conclusion, allow me to tell you that I often contemplated Sophocles' statement (so magnificently presented in French by André Bonnard): "It is not reason never to yield to reason! In flood time you can see how some trees bend, and because they bend, even their twigs are safe, while stubborn trees are torn up, roots and all . . ." (Dudley Fitts-Robert Fitzgerald translation).

Pro Arte   Santiago de Chile, June 2, 1949

(The interview, conducted by Santiago del Campo, took place in Hollywood)[27]

. . . I have never been able to understand Stokowski's mania for employing armies of performers to play Bach and Mozart. This is a monstrosity. All [Stokowski] has managed to do is to distort the character of the music. Bach's Passions, written for 30 people at most, including soloists, choir, and orchestra, are in no need of such boosting . . . I always prefer small, intimate concert halls. Talk about the Metropolitan Opera House terrifies me. . . .

Critics are always . . . trying to bathe themselves in what they call "artistic sentiment." When they ask me if emotion exists in music, I do not know how to reply . . . Of course emotion exists—one always works with emotion—but in art, emotion is understood. The issue is something else: what the Greeks call *Poiesis*: "to know how to do." Music is a matter of technique, culture, and knowledge. It is a finality, as significant as philosophy or mathematics. Emotion is for the audience.

I have never been under a "religious influence." I wrote a Mass and a *Symphony of Psalms*, just as all composers, Mozart, Haydn, Brahms, have employed religious themes, as a problem of form . . . Am I to suppose that after my ballet *Orpheus* the critics will assert that I am searching for the path to the Inferno? . . .

"Classicism" must be broken down into periods: 17th century, 18th century, etc. All great musicians become classical. Contemporary composers? . . . I definitely do not like Messiaen. . . .

If by a miracle—which, fortunately, will never occur—my work were presented to me finished before I had begun it, I would feel profound anguish. *Creating* is the artist's salvation; theories are not. As Paul Valéry once told me: "I prefer the work to the recipe . . ."

[27] Señor del Campo describes his entrance to the Stravinsky residence: ". . . Sunset Boulevard, Ciro's [night club], Earl Carroll, Don Loper, Schwob's drugstore . . . Finally I make out the sign 'Bit of Sweden' and turn on this street, which goes up the mountain. Lawns and gardens replace neon signs . . . and the gates of 1260 North Wetherly . . . open into a garden of flowers, especially roses. In the distance, the Pacific is visible between the trees . . ."

The San Francisco Examiner   December 13, 1950

(The interview was written by Alexander Fried)

At the time when every conflict threatens to flame into a world disaster, one does not have much appetite for projects. But, fortunately, projects do come to mind. Right now I am so terribly busy that I can live artistically within myself . . . Hoping and thinking are two different things. Thinking in this sense has an element of wishfulness. In hope there is no wishful thinking; there is only hope . . .

I wrote *Firebird* and *Petrushka* so long ago that they no longer seem to be particularly mine. When I conduct them, they seem like standard general repertory—as if I were conducting *Shéhérazade* or *Till Eulenspiegel* . . .

The New York Herald Tribune   December 21, 1952

(The interview was written by Jay S. Harrison)

As never before, I am today interested in purely contrapuntal music . . . most of all Heinrich Isaak. He is my hobby, my daily bread. I love him. I study him constantly. And between his musical thinking and writing and my own there is a very close connection. Especially in the part writing . . . I came to him *poco a poco*. It is his contrapuntal mentality that interests me. See—here is the newly published volume of his *Choralis Constantinus, Book III*. A great work. Not a home should be without it . . . especially fascinating for me are the intervals . . . I have been interested in . . . the vertical results that arise from the combinations of intervals. That, by the way, is what is wrong with most twelve-tone composers. They are indifferent to the vertical aspect of music. They are terribly deaf to the logic of vertical combination.

Certain twelve-tone things I like, certain I don't. For instance, I have tremendous respect for the discipline . . . *That* you find nowhere else. But on the other hand, there are too many twelve-tone swindlers working today . . . Not, of course, Schoenberg,[28] Berg, or Webern. These are masters, wonderful musicians, luxury composers. But some others do not hear what they are writing. [My] discipline is tonality. After all, it is not easy to write tonal music. . . .

After I finished *The Rake's Progress*, I had a strong desire to compose another work in which the problem of setting English words to music would reappear but this time in a non-dramatic form. In the Cantata, three of the poems are semi-sacred and the fourth, "Westron Wind," is a love lyric. In all of them my methods are much closer to the distant past than they were years ago . . . I have found marvelous things long before the Baroque. Why is it, do you suppose, that we deny everything in the past upon which the present is founded?

(Later interviews are found in the captions, concluding with the one from 1963 on p. 136.)

[28] In an interview with Stravinsky in July 1952, after the Paris Festival in May, Albert Goldberg of the *Los Angeles Times* quotes the composer saying "*Erwartung* is a wonderful work" (*Times*, July 20).

10

10 *1900s*. Henriette Fyodorovna Malmgren de Bosset (1870–1944?), like her only child, was born on Christmas Day. One of Mme de Bosset's brothers was the Arctic explorer Malmgren. Another was the cellist Eugene Malmgren, who, in 1900, employed the young Igor Stravinsky as piano accompanist. During the Revolution, Artur de Bosset left Russia, but his wife chose to stay. Vera saw her mother for the last time in Paris in December 1925. Mme de Bosset returned to Moscow. In 1938, when Vera last heard from her, she was working in the Karpov Physics and Chemistry Institute. At that time she lived with Vladimir Petrov, at Pokrovsky Boulevard, No. 8, apartment 9. She died during World War II.

11 *1900s*. Artur de Bosset (1867–1937) was a wealthy factory-owner in Kudinovo. One of his ancestors was the Monsieur de Beausset, Prefect of Paris, who brought the portrait of "L'Aiglon" from the Empress to Napoleon before the Battle of Borodino. (This is mentioned in *War and Peace*.) A liberal, who refused the order of St. Stanislas, Artur de Bosset named his daughter after Vera, a "leftist," in Goncharov's *The Precipice*. In 1917, he divorced and married Irena Emilovna Mella, a friend of his first wife. The couple moved to Santiago, Chile, where he died in August 1937. His widow lived in Buenos Aires after his death, and in August 1960, during a trip to Argentina, Vera met her for the first time.

11

12

12 *Christmas 1936*. Moscow. V. I. Petrov (proposing a birthday toast to Vera's mother, his wife). At the other end of the table, the painter Ostrov.

13

14

13 *1900*. Vera de Bosset was born December 25, 1888, Aptekarsky Ostrov, Pesochnaya Ulitsa, 5, St. Petersburg. In 1900 the family moved to Kudinovo, a village about forty-five minutes from Moscow on the Nizhni–Novgorod line, and this photograph shows Vera there with her cat Mashka. Vera remembers that when the Tsar's train went by, soldiers stood on both sides of the tracks pointing their guns toward the houses, the windows of which had to be curtained.

14, 15 *1905*. Moscow. In school uniform. In Kudinovo, Vera's father owned Russia's largest electrical-equipment factory. At age thirteen, Vera entered the Pussell boarding school in Moscow, which she attended for the next four years, with the exception of weekends at home and vacations at home and in Switzerland. School was a trial, except for a *nanya*, who called her "Bossic," and Vera was soon leading a hunger strike to protest about the rations. "Shall I send to Tiestov's for lobster?" the headmistress sarcastically asked her rebellious boarder, who replied that the idea seemed a capital one. In Moscow, Vera pursued her musical studies under David Shor, of the Shor, Krein and Ehrlich "Moscow Trio." She became an accomplished pianist, but soon discovered that her vocation was acting. Her primary interest was in the theater, where she was deeply impressed by the plays of Chekhov, the productions of Stanislavsky, and the performances of Bernhardt, Duse, Isadora Duncan.

15

16

17

18

G. Burger St. Petersbourg

19

16 *1905*. Kudinovo. Vera and her cousin, Vladimir Ivanovich, son of her mother's sister, Olya. He became a professor of radiology at the University of Moscow. After a separation of almost fifty years, the two cousins met in that city in September 1962.

17 *1906*. Kudinovo.

18 *1908*. Hungerford, on the Gulf of Finland. Vera and her mother, sidesaddle; the boy is Vera's cousin, Vladimir Ivanovich Petrov. Vera's mother was her closest companion.

19 *1908*. Graduated *cum laude*, gold-medaled, and certified to teach mathematics and French, Mademoiselle de Bosset hoped to continue her studies in Paris. But the young ladies of her father's acquaintance who had been finished in Parisian schools were distinguished more by their affectations and wanton ways than by their intellectual attainments. The German capital seemed to Vera's father safer and more serious, and, accordingly, she was enrolled in the University of Berlin and sent to a *pension* "kept by a pair of despotic old maids." She returned to Russia both intellectually improved and without affectations, remaining free of them all her life, no doubt being immune to the fault.

20 *1875*. Kiev. Anna Kirilovna Stravinsky (1854–1939), the composer's mother, was born in Kiev. Her mother, Maria Romanovna Kholodovskaya, née Furman, inherited a fortune from her step-grandfather, Fyodor Ivanovich Engel (1770–1837). Maria Romanovna married an impoverished Ukrainian nobleman, Kyril Grigorievich Kholodovsky (1806–1865), and they had four daughters, of whom Anna, the youngest, married F. I. Stravinsky, in Kiev in 1874. She was an excellent pianist with an unusual ability to sight-read music, and she often accompanied her husband. At the beginning of the 1914 war, she was in Switzerland with Igor, the third of her four sons, but she soon returned to Russia. After the war, on April 27, 1920, she applied for permission to visit his family in France, and on June 12, 1922, he obtained a document from the French Department of Foreign Affairs granting this request from the French side. Anna then applied for a year's visa, but was granted one for only six months, and with the stipulation that Stravinsky meet her on the dock at Stettin. Uncertain of the day of her arrival, he spent two months in Berlin, until her passport was finally stamped (Moscow, October 12) "From the République Socialiste Fédérative des Soviets de Russie: Proletarians of all countries unite!" On the 31st, the German Consul General in Petrograd gave her a visa to pass through Germany, on condition that within 24 hours of her arrival she present herself to the Berlin police and remain no longer than ten days. She reached the German capital on November 10, 1922, and thereafter lived in France with Igor's family.

21 *1876*. Kiev. Fyodor Ignatievich Stravinsky (1843–1902). The composer's father was born in the village of Novyi Dvor, in the Minsk District. "Stravinsky" is a Polish name, but his branch of the family lived within the principality of Lithuania. His father—the composer's grandfather—had been an estate manager in Chernigovsky and in the Poltovsky District. F. I. Stravinsky's parents divorced and the boy was brought up, separated from his sister and two brothers, in Mozyr and Nazhin. In 1865, F. I. Stravinsky entered the law school of Vladimir University in Kiev. Three years later he transferred to the Nazhin Lyceum, graduating in the spring of 1869. At that time he was appearing regularly in public as a bass. Between 1870 and 1873, he took singing lessons from Professor K. Everardi at the St. Petersburg Conservatory, and from 1873 to 1876 he sang in the Kiev Opera. Thereafter he became a soloist at the Maryinsky Theater (St. Petersburg), performing on its stage for a quarter of a century. The fame of I. F. Stravinsky was for many years compared to that of F. I. Stravinsky. Thus, after his first

DE MEZER · KIEFF

20

21

22

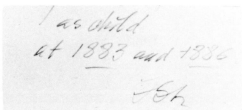

23

concert in Buenos Aires, in 1936, I. F. Stravinsky received the following letter from Constantin Izrastsov, the Father Superior of the Orthodox Church: "To Igor Stravinsky and to Russia's Glory. The thunderous applause and countless ovations reminded me of the days of your father, artist of the St. Petersburg Imperial Theaters, whom we students applauded and followed with just as much excitement and enthusiasm fifty years ago . . ." (April 29, 1936). F. I. Stravinsky's tomb, in Leningrad's Necropolis of the Immortal Masters, is near those of Dostoievsky, Tchaikovsky, Mussorgsky, Rimsky-Korsakov, and Glinka. The grave of Igor Stravinsky's younger brother, Gury, who died in Rumania of peritonitis in 1917, is a part of F. I. Stravinsky's tomb.

22 On June 5, Old Style, 1882, Igor Stravinsky was born in this summer house in Oranienbaum (Lomonosov). The drawing is by his father.

Debussy – Stravinsky
1910
Paris 80 Av. du Bois
chez Debussy

24

25 *Summer 1911.* Russia. Just before
beginning the composition of *Le Sacre du
printemps.*

25

26

27

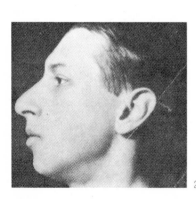

28

29

26 *Spring 1911.* Beaulieu-sur-mer. Stravinsky spent the winter of 1910–11 here, composing *Petrushka*, as he had spent the winter before in an apartment on the English Prospect (now Maklin Prospect), 26/53, St. Petersburg, composing *Firebird.* In November 1910 he went to St. Petersburg to plan the staging of *Petrushka* with Diaghilev, Fokine, Benois and Nijinsky. In January 1911, Stravinsky celebrated his fifth wedding anniversary with a trip to Genoa.

27 *April 16, 1911.* Monte Carlo. With Nijinsky.

28 *1912.* St. Petersburg.

29 *February 1915.* Château d'Oex, Switzerland. Much of *Les Noces* was composed here between January and March 1915.

Paris 1913

30

31, 32 Two photographs by Stravinsky of
Serge Diaghilev. Left, by Lake Geneva,
October 1913. Right, Belle Rive, August 1915.

33 *1912*. Berlin, in the Grunewald. Vera and a student friend. In 1908 Vera entered the University of Berlin as a student in philosophy, science and anatomy. Switching to an art curriculum in her second year, she attended Heinrich Wölfflin's lectures in art history. While in Berlin, she met Robert Shilling, a Balt, and, returning to Moscow, married him in 1912. There, as a pupil in the Nelidova Ballet School, she met Diaghilev and Fokine during one of Diaghilev's visits in search of dancers.

34 *1912*. Moscow. Vera's first husband was a certain Mr. Lury, but since the marriage was soon dissolved, little is known about him. She then married Robert Shilling, who was a compulsive gambler and the newlyweds were constantly in debt. Early in 1913 Vera left him and eloped to Paris with the painter Serge Yurievich Sudeikin, who had been employed by Diaghilev to design the ballet *La Tragédie de Salomé* and to work on the set of *Le Sacre du printemps*. Mikhail Kuzmin described the romance of Vera and Sudeikin in a poem. When Aleksandr Tairov, director of the Kamerny Theater, learned of Vera's passion for the theater and of her desire to join his company, he paid her a visit. Vera candidly admits that he came because he knew that her father was very wealthy. Tairov's company was rehearsing Beaumarchais' *Le Mariage de Figaro*, and Sudeikin wanted her to appear in the production. Since she had studied ballet, he and Tairov created an interpolated Spanish dance for her, and Sudeikin designed a special costume, decorated with tiny stars. During his courtship, Sudeikin had referred to himself as Figaro, but since the name Susanna did not suit Vera Arturovna, he called her Donna Anna. Their rendezvous took place in the great cathedrals of the Kremlin, the Uspenki and Blagovescenki. Kuzmin mentions the black "*subka*" that she wore. When Sudeikin obtained a separation from his wife Olga Glebova, he and Vera moved to St. Petersburg (on March 15, 1916) where they took an apartment above the Prival Komediantov, a café prominent in the lives of poets and artists. Kuzmin was a regular guest at the apartment and the three of them would visit the café to see friends. Kuzmin was captivated by Vera's intelligence and charm, and as an Easter gift for her, he wrote the poem *Cuzaja* (so called because it is the narrative of someone else's love affair told from Sudeikin's point of view). The manuscript, which she still has, was presented to her by Kuzmin and is dated "1916. April. Easter." Later in 1916, Vera and Sudeikin resided in an apartment on the Ekaterinsky Canal. They were still living there when Rasputin was murdered (December 1916). As a result of being forced to lie in the snow in a bullet-strafed street during the Revolution of March 1917, Vera became ill and, as soon as she was able to travel, returned to Moscow. Sudeikin's father, a former police official in St. Petersburg, was one of the Bolsheviks' first victims, and Serge and Vera soon joined the exodus to the Crimea, where, on February 11, 1918, they were married. (The marriage was dissolved by a Boston court, March 5, 1940, by which date the Sudeikins had not seen each other for more than fifteen years. On August 5, 1945, to satisfy a Los Angeles court that was ruling on the Stravinskys' application for citizenship, the composer fabricated a statement that his wife's marriage to Sudeikin had been terminated on February 20, 1920, in Tiflis.)

35 *1915*. Moscow. In riding habit for a film. Vera did not go to ballet school to become a ballerina. "I was too tall and too late-starting for that," she says. "What I wanted was to acquire poise, be able to move gracefully, and learn something about bodily expression. I considered ballet to be good basic training for an actress, which is what I had determined to become."

34

33

36 *1915.* Moscow. Vera "dead," still from a film. The theater was Vera's greatest delight. It was the heyday of the ballet, of Russian opera—the first opera she saw was Tchaikovsky's *The Little Slippers*—of Stanislavsky. In the first two plays she attended, she had the astronomical luck to see Eleonora Duse and Sarah Bernhardt. Imitating these actresses in drama classes at school, Vera made a hit by fainting in the Bernhardt manner: "I went down like *that* [gestures] and there I was, *par terre.*"

37 *1915.* Moscow. As Helen in Protozanov's *War and Peace*, Vera's most important film role. In 1914, Vera was engaged as an actress at Tairov's Kamerny Theater. She also played in films, and one of her partners was Marius Petipa, son of the choreographer of *Swan Lake.* "Once I was at the movies with a boyfriend and he said, 'Why aren't you in movies?' I said, 'I don't know, of course I could be.' So he got the name of a film director from the doorman, we looked in the book and phoned him." Vera went and said she'd like to be in films. "He looked at me, I looked at him, nicely, you know. I said, 'I can always play a little bit, silent. I have marvelous dresses, my mother buys them in Paris. I am very sportif, I ride and play tennis.'" Russsian actresses then were, Madame explained, not at all sportif and had to wear their own clothes in films. "So I drove four horses in a park in *War and Peace.* And I wore my own tailleur, very nice." Nobody knew about it; the family found out when they saw the picture. Madame recalled with glee their cries: "'She looks like Vera! Is, it possible?' It was shocking to be an actress then, remember. I am 90 now, I was eighteen or nineteen then." (Lesley Thornton, from *Harper's & Queen Magazine*, London, October 1979.)

36

38 *1917.* Osip Mandelstam's original manuscript of *Tristia* No. 3. (See next page for a translation.)

"[In the summer of 1917] we stayed in Alushta . . . Suddenly Osip Mandelstam appeared . . . We took him out to the vineyards—'We have nothing else to show you.' And we had nothing to serve him except tea with honey. No bread. But the talk was lively, not about politics at all but about art, literature, painting. A witty, cheerful, charming conversationalist. We were delighted by his visit. 'Come again. We're so glad to see you.' August 11: he did come and brought us his poem.

"We wanted to see him again, his animated expression, to hear his conversational enthusiasm. He wore a raincoat; I don't think he even had a suit; and he looked hungry, but we could not offer him anything—there was literally nothing; we ourselves were half-starving. I remember that there was a meat patty left over from dinner and hidden in the dresser 'just in case.' He stood in front of the dresser for a long time, looked over the sketches pinned to the wall, and I thought, 'We must give him that meat patty; he probably senses its existence,' but I didn't—it was intended for Seryozha [Sudeikin] before he went to bed.'' (From Vera Stravinsky's diary.)

38

39

The thread of golden honey flowed from the bottle
so languorously our hostess had time to say—
here in mournful Tauris where our fates have cast us—
we will not be bored. She glanced over her shoulder.

Everywhere the rites of Bacchus, as if the whole world
contained only guards and dogs. As you walk you see no one.
And the peaceful days roll on like heavy barrels. Far off
in the ancient rooms are voices which you neither understand
    nor answer.

After tea we came out into the great brown garden.
Dark blinds lowered like eyelids on the windows.
We walk by white columns to see the grapes. Beyond them
airy glass has been poured over the drowsing mountains.

The vines, I said, live on like ancient battles,
with leafy horsemen tangled in skirmishes.
Here in stony Tauris is an art of Hellas: here, rusted,
are the golden acres, the noble ranks.

Meanwhile silence stands in the white room like a spinning
    wheel.
It smells of vinegar, paint, and wine cool from the cellar.
Do you remember, in the Grecian house, the wife they all
    loved?
Not Helen, the other? And how she embroidered time?

Golden fleece, where are you, golden fleece?
The whole journey a heaving of the sea's waves.
Leaving his ship and its sea-wearied sails,
Odysseus returned, filled with space and time.

39 *1918*. Yalta. Vera by Sudeikin. With the approach of the Red Army in the spring of 1919, Vera and Sudeikin sailed for Constantinople. She recalls that Vladimir Nabokov's father was on the same Yalta pier, as well as the dowager Empress, who was rescued by an English cruiser. The Sudeikins' ark was more modest, a mere thirty-footer, loaded with oil drums. A heavy storm came up, and, after many queasy hours, the couple was put ashore at Batum, at the wrong end of the Black Sea. From there they journeyed to Tiflis, where camels were still the main means of transportation in the bazaar. For the next year, Tiflis was their home, a happy one, to judge from Vera's diaries, despite the Revolution. In Tiflis, the Polish artist Sigismund Valeshevski drew her portrait, and Serge Gorodetsky dedicated several poems to her, as well as painting watercolor album portraits for her—of himself, Blok, Kuzmin, Balmont, Biely, Brussov, Remizov, Sologub. She also met Gurdjieff, who purchased two of her antique rugs. A description of the Sudeikins in Tiflis by Titian Tabidze, the Georgian poet, appeared in *Literary Georgia*, Nos. 10–11, Tiflis, 1967. According to Tabidze, the Sudeikins lived in a basement room in Griboyedova Street, but spent much of their time in the Café Chimerion, which had been founded by Sudeikin and a group of poets, and embellished with murals by him and two other painters. Another café frequented by the Sudeikins was the Darbazi. Tabidze remarks that "Sudeikin was always with his muse, Vera Arturovna Lury-Sudeikina, whose beauty was such that everyone in Tiflis would stop and look at her. His paintings were always variations of her face." Tabidze identifies Vrubel and Nikolai Yevrainova (the stage-director) as "among the Sudeikins' closest Tiflis friends." In May 1920, to buy passage to Marseilles for herself and Sudeikin, Vera sold her diamond-with-pearl earrings for 3,000 Kerensky rubles. In company with the painter Savely Sorin and Prince Melikov, the Sudeikins set sail for Constantinople and France on the French steamer S.S. *Souirah*. A few hours after the departure from Batum, Georgian pirates, who had boarded the ship during a coaling stop there, and mingled with the passengers, robbed the diamonds of Mrs. Haskell, wife of the American Commissioner in Transcaucasia, and relieved the other passengers of their valuables—except Vera, to whom the admiring buccaneer chieftain gave a louis d'or as a talisman. (She still has it.) The bandits, who landed at the Turkish port of Riza, were captured by a French destroyer and tried and convicted of piracy in Marseilles. (Vera and Igor saw the S.S. *Souirah* in Marseilles in the summer of 1930.)

Vera's only surviving friends from the Crimea–Caucasus period are Boris Kochno, Varvara Karinskaya ("Varinka" and "Verinka"), and Salomeya Nikolaevna Halperin (née Princess Andronikov). Salomeya and Vera are the same age (ninety-three) and they still see each other during Vera's visits to London—Salomeya lives in Chelsea Gardens—and still exchange recollections of Osip Mandelstam, who had been in love with both of them. (He wrote his poem No. 86 for Salomeya in 1916.) Salomeya had been a friend of Ashenia Miliukov and her wealthy husband, and in Tiflis, in the hot summer of 1919, Salomeya and the Sudeikins vacationed in Borzhom—to which they journeyed on the Miliukovs' private train. (Such, such were the hardships of the Revolution—for some.) Later, in Paris and London between the wars, Salomeya became a friend of Stravinsky's, but between 1938 and the 1950s, they met only once—in New York on February 5, 1945.

40 *1916*. Petrograd. Silhouette of Vera by Anna Akhmatova, on the other side of which she wrote "*Byaka*" ("naughty girl"); the poet had been in love with Sudeikin and had lost him to Vera. In a notebook of reminiscences of Osip Mandelstam, Ahkmatova wrote: "The lady in his poem [*Tristia* No. 3] who looked over her shoulder was *Byaka*. At that time she was a friend of Sudeikin. Later she married Igor Stravinsky." (*Works*, Vol. II, Inter-Language Literary Associates, West Germany, 1967.) When Akhmatova received an honorary D. Litt. at Oxford, in June 1965, she brought the silhouette with her and entrusted it to Sir Isaiah Berlin to give to Mme Stravinsky. Late in life, Akhmatova wrote: "We now know that Stravinsky's destiny did not remain chained to the 1910s, that his work became the highest expression of the 20th century's spirit."

41 *1921*. Paris. Vera, at the time she met Stravinsky. Soon after the Sudeikins arrived in Paris, in May 1920, Diaghilev called on his old friend and was captivated by his wife. One day in February 1921, Diaghilev invited Vera to a dinner at which Stravinsky was present. Of this first meeting, in an Italian restaurant in Montmartre, Vera recalls that the composer was "the wittiest, most amusing man I had ever met . . ." She had a pack of cards with her that night, and she told the composer's fortune—presumably saying something about the queen of hearts.

40

41

42

42 *February 1920.* At the home, near Paris, of
Jacques Rouché, director of the Paris Opéra.
L. to r., Ernest Ansermet, Leonide Massine,
Diaghilev, Tamara Karsavina, Stravinsky,
Misia Sert.

43 *Autumn 1920.* Paris. With Misia Sert, Coco
Chanel, and José Maria Sert.

43

44 *April 1921.* Madrid. With Diaghilev.

45 *June 1921.* Near London. With Arthur Rubinstein.

46 *Summer 1921.* ''Cottage à l'Argenté,'' Anglet (near Biarritz), Stravinsky in the windowsill of his studio. This is the first picture of himself that he inscribed ''Vierochka—Igor.''

A. JACOVLEFF. — Portrait de Mme Soudeikine.

48

49

50

48 *April 1921.* Seville. Boris Kochno, Holy Week celebrant, and Serge Diaghilev. Photograph by Stravinsky, the shadow of whose hat is at the bottom of the picture. Vera knew Kochno, the young poet, in the Crimea, and she had introduced him to Diaghilev in Paris two months before this photograph was taken.

49 *December 1921.* ''Villa des Rochers,'' Biarritz.

50 *Summer 1921.* Anglet.

51 ''Boris Kochno
Dear Vera Arturovna on her day [Vera's
   'name day,' September 30, 1921],
     Da, da, da!''

The inscription in Stravinsky's hand, below
   Kochno's inscription, says:
     ''but not Da-da
       To Vera''
   [and, after the music] ''I don't remember the
   rest.''

52 ''Pronounce the Russian letter A as ie—
everywhere

Automobile accident
I drank cognac
Gardes de Marines have left
With the grasshopper on the sofa—
Discussing opera

To a Lady
This charming
This beautiful
This dear
Vera Sudeikina.

From *Svadebka* [*Les Noces*, 127 through the
second measure of 128] Igor Stravinsky, Paris
1921.''

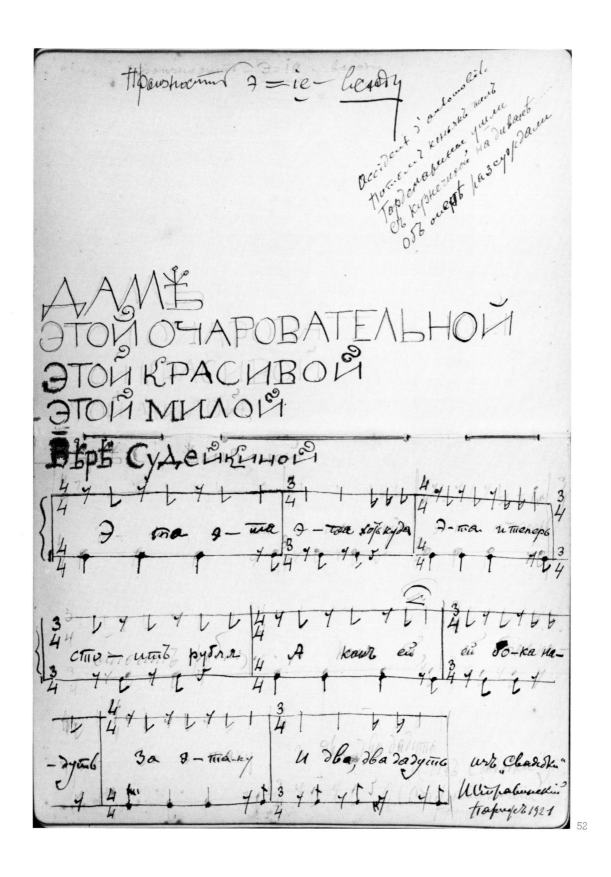

53 *November 1921*. London. The Alhambra Theater. Vera was the Queen in Diaghilev's production of *The Sleeping Princess (The Sleeping Beauty)*. Her costume is now in the Metropolitan Museum of Art in New York.

54, 55 *1922*. Portrait by Bakst. The two notes from the painter read: "To the Beautiful Queen of *Sleeping Beauty*, Vera Arturovna Sudeikina. Your loyal subject, Lev Bakst, London, November 27, 1921''; and, "I, the undersigned, hereby certify that, following the premiere of the 'Maria Kuznetsova Theater,' I have agreed to paint, to the best of my abilities, a portrait of Vera Arturovna. Lev Bakst, May 23, 1922.'' Bakst had wanted to do the decor for Stravinsky's *Mavra*, and when Diaghilev chose Survage instead, Bakst broke with the composer. *Mavra* also precipitated the separation of Vera and Sudeikin: he forbade her to attend the piano preview of the opera, to which Stravinsky had invited her, and though she did not go, the next day she left Sudeikin permanently. In the summer she moved her Paris fashion accessories shop to Deauville, where the establishment was called "Tula-Vera" (Tula Danilova was the daughter of a former high government official at Tsarskoe Selo); it reopened in the autumn in Paris, 6, rue Euler. On August 19, 1922, Sudeikin went to America to fulfill commissions as a stage designer for the Metropolitan Opera, and Vera and Gabrielle Picabia (ex-wife of the painter) shared an apartment at 82, rue des Petits-Champs.

"LA BELLE AU BOIS DORMANT"

Lettre à Serge de Diaghilew

Cher ami,

Je suis heureux de te voir monter cette œuvre capitale : *La Belle au Bois Dormant*, de notre cher grand Tchaïkowsky. J'en suis doublement heureux. Cela m'est d'abord une joie personnelle, car cette œuvre me semble être l'expression la plus authentique de l'époque de notre vie russe que nous appelons la « période de Petersbourg », gravée dans ma mémoire avec la vision matinale des traîneaux impériaux d'Alexandre III, l'énorme Empereur et son énorme cocher, et la joie immense qui m'attendait le soir : le spectacle de *La Belle au Bois Dormant*. C'est ensuite ma grande satisfaction de musicien de voir présentée une œuvre d'un caractère si direct, à un moment où tant de gens qui ne sont ni simples, ni naïfs, ni spontanés, recherchent dans leur art, la simplicité, la « pauvreté » et la spontanéité.

Tchaïkowsky possédait la grande puissance *mélodique*, centre de gravitation de chaque symphonie, opéra ou ballet qu'il composait. Il m'est absolument indifférent que la qualité de sa mélodie soit parfois de valeur inégale. Le fait est qu'il fut créateur de *mélodie*, don extrêmement rare et précieux. Chez nous, Glinka le possédait aussi ; et pas autant, les autres...

Et voilà qui n'est pas allemand...

Les Allemands fabriquaient de la musique avec des thèmes et des leit-motifs, les substituant à des mélodies.

La musique de Tchaïkowsky, ne paraissant pas à tout le monde spécifiquement russe, est souvent plus profondément russe que celle qui, depuis long-

LA BELLE AU BOIS DORMANT

(Dessin inédit de Léon BAKST)

LE MEDECIN

temps a reçu l'étiquette facile du pittoresque moscovite.

Cette musique est tout autant russe que le vers de Pouchkine, ou le chant de Glinka. Ne cultivant pas spécialement dans son art « l'âme paysanne russe », Tchaïkowsky puisait *inconsciemment* dans les vraies sources populaires de notre race.

Et à quel point ses préférences dans la musique ancienne et de son temps

étaient-elles caractéristiques! Il adorait Mozart, Couperin, Glinka, Bizet : voilà qui ne laisse nul doute sur la qualité de son goût. Chose étrange, chaque fois qu'un musicien russe s'influençait de cette culture latino-slave et voyait clairement la frontière entre l'Autrichien catholique Mozart tourné vers Beaumarchais, et l'Allemand protestant Beethoven, incliné vers Gœthe, le résultat était marquant...

L'exemple convaincant de la grande puissance créatrice de Tchaïkowsky est sans aucun doute le ballet de *La Belle au Bois Dormant*. Cet homme cultivé, connaisseur de vieilles chansons et de l'ancienne musique française, quand il s'agit de présenter le siècle de Louis XIV, ne s'occupe aucunement de recherches archéologiques et recrée le caractère de l'époque par son propre langage musical, préférant les anachronismes involontaires et vivants aux pastiches conscients et travaillés : qualité propre aux seuls grands créateurs.

Je viens de relire la partition de ce ballet : j'en ai orchestré quelques morceaux, qui étaient restés non instrumentés et jamais joués. J'ai passé quelques journées de plaisir extrême en y retrouvant toujours le même sentiment de fraîcheur, d'invention, d'ingéniosité et de puissance. Et je souhaite vivement que cette œuvre soit sentie par les auditeurs de tous pays, comme elle l'est par moi, musicien russe.

Bien à toi.

Igor Stravinsky.

Dessin inédit de Léon BAKST).

LA BELLE AU BOIS DORMANT

LA REINE ET UN PAGE

Прекрасной
Королевъ изъ „Спящей Красавицы"
— Вѣрѣ Артуровнѣ Судейкиной —
Верноподданный Левъ Бакстъ
London 27 Novembre 1921.

Симъ удостовѣряю, что поетъ
первый премьеръ „Театра Марiи
Кузнецовой" обязуюсь исполнить, ежели
мочь, художественно портретъ Вѣры
Артуровны, въ чемъ и подписуюсь
Левъ Бакстъ
23 Мая 1922

54   55

55

56

56, 57 *April 1923*. Monte Carlo. Igor, by Vera
. . . and . . . Vera, by Igor.

58 *April 1923*. Monte Carlo. Between
rehearsals for *Les Noces*. L. to r., Svevelod
Grigoriev, Serge Grigoriev, Mme Grigoriev
(Liubov Tchernicheva), Lydia Sokolova,
Stravinsky, Vera Nemchinova, Vera Sudeikina
(with parasol), Stanislas Idzikowski. (The
woman behind Stravinsky is unidentified.) At
the time of this photograph, Vera played the
role of the Bride in *Les Noces*, but she was
obliged to withdraw because of illness.

59 *1923*. Monte Carlo.

60 *June 1923*. Paris. Dedication of the title-
page of *Les Noces*. Stravinsky has written, at
the top, "Vera and Igor, [their] *Svadebka*
[marriage]."

58

59

ВѢРѢ—ИГОРЬ

Парижъ іюнь 1923г.

СВАДЕБКА

РУССКІЯ
ХОРЕОГРАФИЧЕСКІЯ СЦЕНЫ
съ
ПѢНІЕМЪ И МУЗЫКОЙ

соч.

ИГОРЯ СТРАВИНСКАГО

60

57

61

62

63

61 *1923*. At Fontainebleau.

62 *June 1923*. St. Cloud. Photo by Gabrielle Picabia. Mme Picabia was in charge of a "Paris Press Information Bureau" for a New York company. She shared the apartment in rue des Petits-Champs with Mme Sudeikina from 1922 to 1926. Mme Picabia accompanied Igor and Vera to Antwerp for a concert in 1924.

63 *October 1923*. Quai Voltaire. Photograph by Vera.

64 *1923*. At St. Cloud. In 1923, Savely Sorin, a good society portrait artist, painted Vera's portrait.

65 *June 1923*. A roadside near Chantilly.

66 *June 1923*. Paris. Photo by Man Ray.

64

65

66

67 *End of September 1924.* Nice. In the Queen's Hotel, before moving to 167 Boulevard Carnot. Stravinsky spent the first two weeks in September in Paris obtaining visas for his forthcoming concert tour. On September 10 he wrote from there to his concert agent in Berlin, Dr. Peter Sirota, saying that it had been necessary to make a special trip from Biarritz for this purpose, and that another week would be required.

The letters home (Leningrad) of Tanya, the composer's niece, between April 1925 and February 1926, provide many vignettes of life in the Stravinsky home in Nice. She came to France to study secretarial skills and lived with the composer's family. In the first letter after seeing her uncle, she remarked that he "gives me some of his liquors to drink, though normally no one is allowed to touch them but him. He taught me how to smoke and in our conversations he uses improper language. . . . But when Uncle left, everything seemed empty" (April 19). On July 20–21, she chronicled the arrival of "another new gadget, the very latest pianola. We also have rolls containing a lot of Uncle's music. He turned on the keyboard and out came the most perfect sound. Usually the notes are photographed as you play them, but Uncle has done it all mechanically. When you follow the notes on the little roll, you can actually see how everything is put together. I can already read the music almost as well by the little holes as by the notes. Pleyel also sent us 15 rolls containing fox-trots so that we can dance. We have all learned to operate the machine by now, but not everyone can manage all of the nuances. I have heard Uncle perform *Petrushka, Firebird, Pulcinella, The Nightingale,* the Concertino, *Les Noces,* the Octet and some Russian songs."

68, 69, 70 *November 5, 1924.* Warsaw.

71 *November 7, 1924.* Warsaw. Stravinsky, about to play his Sonata (completed October 21) for Gregor Fitelberg (leaning on the piano, to the composer's right), a couple called Mayer (behind Vera), and Alexander Borovsky (seated next to Stravinsky). Fitelberg conducted the first performance of *Mavra* (Paris, June 3, 1922) and Diaghilev's London revival of *The Sleeping Beauty.* Borovsky (1889–1968) met Stravinsky in Paris in 1922, and once performed the "8 Easy Pieces" with him. On October 27, 1924, Stravinsky wrote from Nice to N. A. Aloukhen, of the Russischer Musik Verlag in Berlin: "Tomorrow I am going to Paris where I will fetch the parts from Oeberg for the Octet,

67

Concerto, and perhaps *The Song of the Nightingale,* then leave for Warsaw Thursday night. On Friday evening, I will pass through Berlin (without leaving the train: North Express, Friedrichstrasse Station) en route to Warsaw, where I must rehearse Saturday morning November 1. I would be very pleased if you could come to see me at the station in Berlin. (You will find me in the sleeping-car, Paris–Warsaw.) If Sirota does not answer you and you do not know how to manage concerning the parts for *Petrushka,* bring them to me, and I will take them with me, but only on condition that you cannot find Sirota, since I already have too much music with me, which is both embarrassing and

heavy." In Warsaw, Stravinsky and Vera stayed at the Hotel Bristol. On their first Saturday evening in the city, they attended a performance of the *Countess Maritza.* Stravinsky rehearsed on the 1st, 2nd, 3rd, and 4th. The program of the 4th, repeated on the 6th, consisted of the *Pulcinella* Suite, Octet, *Petrushka,* conducted by Stravinsky, and the Concerto, played by him and conducted by Fitelberg. After the concert Igor and Vera attended "A big dinner with the former Polish aristocracy, Countess Rjevoutzki, Potocki, Lubomirski, and others" (V.S.'s diary). On November 8, Vera and Igor left for Prague, where Stravinsky appeared in a concert.

68

69

70

71

72, 73 In January 1925, Stravinsky experienced a public but incomplete meeting with Sudeikin on the stage of the Metropolitan Opera during a double bill of *Petrushka*—for which Sudeikin designed the sets—and *The Nightingale*. Acknowledging the applause for his ballet, Stravinsky started on stage, suddenly saw Sudeikin approaching from the opposite side, froze, bowed alone, departed rapidly. On March 29, 1925, the *Philadelphia Inquirer* devoted a page of its Sunday sensation space to the feud between Stravinsky and Sudeikin,

illustrating the story with a photograph of Vera, identified by the newspaper, no doubt for protection against libel, as "Sonia." Nothing in the article is true, needless to say, Vera having outgrown her ambition for a career in the theater before she met Stravinsky.

On May 14, 1925, Tanya wrote to her parents: "Uncle took a dislike to America and Americans and he says that nowhere has he encountered more stupid and boring people." "Uncle" revised this judgment during his tour

of 1935, during which time Sudeikin tried unsuccessfully to mend his relationship with his wife's lover.

In the same letter, Tanya described the Steinway birthday party in New York, January 11, 1925, as told to her by "Uncle": "All the great musical figures were invited: Josef Hofmann, Alexander Siloti, Sergei Rachmaninov . . . At the end of the banquet, a fantastic chocolate cake in the shape of a piano was brought out, with an open conductor's stand and [Uncle's] name written on the notes. What a pity that the cake was eaten then and there."

Tragedy Of the Famous Artist's Lost Wife

Serge Soudeikine, unselfishly painting the scenery that contributed so much to the American triumph of Stravinsky's ballet-pantomime, "Petrouchka"

Unhappy Serge Soudeikine---Deserted by His Beloved Sonia Because She Admired the Genius of Stravinsky, the Great Musical Composer, More Than His

Igor Stravinsky, the composer, whose genius had such an irresistible fascination for his former friend's wife

Mme. Sonia Soudeikine, who wanted a career so badly that she deserted the husband she thought could never give her one

One of the scenes for "Petrouchka," with whose glowing colors Soudeikine mingled tears of bitter regret for his lost wife

A "Petrouchka" costume, designed and executed by Serge Soudeikine

THE outstanding novelty of the past season at the Metropolitan Opera House in New York, was, as all music lovers know, the very elaborate revival of Igor Stravinsky's "Petrouchka," the musical ballet-pantomime, which is considered one of the most original creations of the modern operatic stage.

While the ultra-modern music of Stravinsky was much admired and praised, almost everybody was agreed that a large part of the triumph "Petrouchka" scored was due to the remarkable scenery and costumes which Serge Soudeikine, the famous Russian scenic artist, came to America especially to design and execute.

But of all the thousands who clapped their hands and drew long breaths of delight over the brilliant artistry of these costumes and settings probably not more than two or three knew that they formed a monument to the great tragedy of the painter's life—that with their glowing colors he had mingled bitter tears of regret over the loss of the beautiful wife whom he loved even more than his art.

The facts of this tragedy have just become known in New York's Russian colony and they show what a tremendous self-sacrifice was involved in Soudeikine's coming to this country and, by linking his genius with Stravinsky's, making the latter's ballet a far more triumphant success than it otherwise might have been.

For Igor Stravinsky is the man Soudeikine could blame for his lost wife. It was her admiration for the composer's genius—and, many suspect, a still deeper feeling for the man himself—which led this restless, ambitious beauty to leave her husband and declare she could not bear to live with him any longer.

As she has recently confessed, she looks upon Stravinsky as her artistic soul mate—feels that he is a man far better fitted than Soudeikine to sympathize with the aspirations of her genius and gratify her desire to express herself.

These surprising revelations of the tragedy which has fallen on the artist's life explain why he and the composer have so studiously avoided each other here in America, although their talents were united in the production of the Metropolitan's greatest novelty. Until within the last few days none of their friends were able to explain this attitude, for it was well known that the two men had once been on the friendliest terms.

Soudeikine arrived here to begin his work for "Petrouchka" several weeks before Stravinsky. But when the latter landed Soudeikine was not one of the throng that gathered at the pier to bid him welcome. Nor did the composer hasten to the artist's studio to inspect the progress of his work for "Petrouchka" and congratulate him on its beauty.

When both men were invited to be guests of honor at a reception at Vincent Astor's home, Soudeikine promptly pleaded illness and remained away. And Stravinsky withheld his acceptance of the invitation until he was sure that Soudeikine was not going to be present.

The gulf that separated the two became so noticeable that one of Soudeikine's friends took courage to ask the reason for it.

"What is the explanation of your strange attitude toward your former friend?" was the way he framed his question.

"'Petrouchka,'" was the artist's reply; "and perhaps the slap of a whimsical fate."

For a long time Soudeikine refused to add anything to these cryptic words. But at length another friend, both inquisitive and eager to be of sympathetic service, coaxed him into unveiling the secret of the burden which weighed with tragic heaviness on his heart.

"I have come to the conclusion," said Soudeikine, "that destiny plays a greater role in a man's success or failure than is generally thought. Until a few months ago, I thought my aspiring ego was everything, and that I was the complete master of my public career and my private happiness. But no more."

He paused, took the portrait of a pretty woman from his portfolio and handed it reverently to his friend.

"This girl," he went on, "was my wife. I thought she would, remain so forever. But a wicked fate came and separated us. She is no longer mine."

"But what has 'Petrouchka' to do with your losing her?" interrupted the friend.

"It has this much, in fact, everything. Her ambition was the stage, preferably rather than his. But I cannot yet bring in a ballet like this of Stravinsky's,

which she admired as much as I. She wanted to have a career of her own. Besides being a wonderful woman she is a wonderful actress.

"She looked up to me as at a feminine god in my perfect knowledge of stage art. As I now realize she hoped in her heart that besides being a husband I might be at the same time a guide and helper to the artistic career she craved.

"But success in art, as in everything else, is a slow climbing over one obstacle after another. It happened that I was unable to make enough money to have my own theatre and paint only what I wanted. I made a good living, but it was not enough to provide the opportunities my wife wanted and expected.

"I came to America and was successful, but still was unable to accumulate a fortune. When I returned to Paris I found, to my great grief and amazement, the woman I loved had left me.

"Long an admirer of Stravinsky, she had become one of his ablest enthusiastic disciples. She was fascinated not only by his genius but by the man himself. She felt convinced that through his art she could find a surer, easier way to the artistic success she coveted than through mine. She told me she must make her own career in her own way and that she could no longer be my wife.

"I went again to America, amazed and heartbroken by the blow that had fallen so unexpectedly on me. Will the woman I married ever wake to the realization that there is something more precious in life than money or artistic fame? That is the question. If she ever does I hope she will come back to me for I love her still.

"If I did not love her I never would have accepted the contract to design the scenery and costumes for 'Petrouchka.' I did it because I hoped it would please her to have me offering my talents on the shrine of the musical genius she admires. Also, I wanted to see her face. Also, I wanted to see her face, that my art, the art which she scorns as not good enough for her vaulting ambitions, was capable of dividing the public's attention with the art of Stravinsky which she thinks so unapproachable.

"I bear Stravinsky no malice. The whole tragedy was of Sonia's making rather than his. But I cannot yet bring myself to resume anything like my old relations with the famous musical composer who has exerted such an overpowering fascination on the woman I love."

Soon after Soudeikine confided this account of his love tragedy to his friend there reached New York from Paris, through intimate friends of Mme. Soudeikine, her version of this unusual real-life drama.

"Perhaps I was always more of an artist than a woman. At any rate, the artistic part of my ego is now in the ascendancy over my femininity. And this was why I could not continue living with Serge.

"I believe in aesthetic companionship, but that seemed to have no appeal for my husband. He wanted only a loving wife and was continually ignoring my ambitions as an artist.

"My intuition told me that in Stravinsky I could find the sympathy and assistance in my ambitions which my husband denied me. I was carried away by my admiration for the great composer and his musical achievements. I became a firm upholder of all his ultra-modern theories, and worshipped his genius. I doubt if any one else ever has done.

"If I could have the benefit of his advice, if I could some day become the star of one of his marvelous ballets—that, I thought, would give me just the opportunity I have long sought to express my aesthetic feelings and win fame. It was this ambition, together with discouragement over my husband's lack of financial success, that drove me from him.

"Stravinsky has been so kind to me. He promised to take me to America with him to see the opening performance of 'Petrouchka.' But when I heard that Serge was designing the scenery and costumes for the ballet I could not bear to go to New York. I remained in Paris not because I was afraid of failing in love with my husband again, but because I know he still loves me and I did not want to wound him any more than I can help. I think it was

really heroic of him to undertake the scenery and costumes for 'Petrouchka' when he knew that I admired Stravinsky's genius more than his.

"Perhaps some day I may return to Serge—who knows? If he should acquire a theatre of his own and should promise me the aesthetic companionship and fling at fame which I crave, it would make all the difference in the world in my feelings toward him. But, as things are now, I believe I was wise in deserting him and starting to work out my artistic destiny under the guidance of Stravinsky."

Mme. Soudeikine's explanation of her conduct was soon common property with the gossips of the New York Russian colony. The other day some one repeated it to Soudeikine.

"Women are heartless creatures," was Soudeikine's comment, "and live only for their emotional egos. She left me because Stravinsky's fame could do more for her than my modest studio life. I thought to please her by stifling my sorrow and producing the scenery for 'Petrouchka.' But, if my work is received with the favor I hope it will be, I doubt if she is at all pleased. She would, I think, be heartbroken to see me lifted to anything like the pedestal on which Igor Stravinsky stands.

"The worst of it is that in spite of everything, I still love Sonia. What a tragedy it is that her ambition should have made her so utterly selfish and heartless!"

The third corner of what is believed a remarkable human triangle is the only one that maintains complete silence. Igor Stravinsky, busy with his American concert tour, is ready to discuss at great length his musical theories and many other topics. But, concerning his relations with his one-time friend, the great scenic painter and the latter's beautiful wife, he has not a word to say.

(Copyright, 1925)

Historic Gun

In the Imperial War Museum in London, is to be seen the gun of H. M. S. Lance, from which was fired the first naval shot in the Great War. This ship, with two companions, came into contact with the German mine-layer Koenigen Luise, and sank her, on August 5, 1914.

75 *August 1925.* In the Alpes-Maritimes. On Igor's return from the United States in March, Vera met him at the ship and they went directly to Barcelona, where Igor had a concert. He did not see his wife in Nice until April 7. On June 13, the composer left Nice for Paris, where, at the end of July, he purchased a Renault. In August, Igor, Vera, his son Theodore, and a chauffeur returned to Nice in the car. A letter from Tanya says that the trip took almost four days, including a delay caused by a storm in the Alpes-Maritimes: "Aunt Katya was terribly worried while they were en route, but Uncle sent two telegrams every day."

76 *September 6, 1925.* Venice. On September 20, 1925, Tanya wrote to her parents: "Uncle has just returned to Nice from Venice. A real miracle took place there. While he was still here at home he had begun to develop an abscess under his fingernail. The situation remained the same on the road, but he was hoping that somehow he might be able to play, since the concert could not be rescheduled. The night before his appearance, the finger pained him so much that he could not touch it. Going on stage the next day, he approached the audience, showed his finger, said he would only be able to play with the other nine, and begged indulgence. Uncle then sat down at the piano, unwound the bandage, and performed his Sonata with all ten fingers, the abscessed one having been miraculously healed and not hurting him at all."

75

74 *1924.* Paris. Photograph by Lipnitzki. In April 1924, Marguerite Beriza commissioned Vera to make costumes for the Paris premiere of *Histoire du soldat.*

76

77

78

77 *September 1925.* Venice. With Werner Reinhart, Stravinsky's Maecenas at the time of *Histoire du soldat* and close friend thereafter. (The Reinhart collection in Winterthur includes the principal manuscripts of *Histoire du soldat*, *Les Noces*, and the Three Pieces for Clarinet.) Stravinsky wrote to Reinhart at the beginning of October 1925: "The photographs from Venice came out admirably. Would it be indiscreet to ask you to send me another one of each? I sent these to Mme Sudeikina, who asks me to convey her best greetings to you." Igor and Vera spent some of their time in Venice with the Princesse de Polignac and some with Arthur Rubinstein. But since Arnold Schoenberg was also in the city and was also a friend of Reinhart's, one regrets that the two composers were not brought together, and that Stravinsky did not hear Schoenberg's Serenade twenty-five years before it made so powerful an impression on him in Los Angeles.

This photograph was taken by Reinhart's protegée, Alma Moodie, the Australian violinist. From Venice, Igor and Vera went to Florence. On the return to France, Stravinsky wrote to Reinhart from Genoa, September 18, the day on which *Oedipus Rex* was conceived.

78 *February 1926.* Marseilles. With Jean Cocteau. Stravinsky's Leningrad niece Tanya, who was living with his family in 1925–26, wrote home August 22–23 (1925): "This evening we had a guest, Jean Cocteau, a talented writer who also draws wonderful caricatures. He stayed to dinner and talked a great deal. . . . I had a fantastic time listening to him, but Aunt Katya does not like having guests. It is a torment to her to have to play the role of hostess and in the end she is very tired. . . . God, how happy I would be in her place! I would not avoid Uncle's friends and, unlike Aunt Katya, I would go everywhere with him."

79

80

Concertgebouw
Amsterdam
2 mars 1926

81

79 *1926*. Near Paris, in their new Hotchkiss. On May 26, 1926, Tanya wrote home from Paris: "Uncle telephoned me on Sunday and we went for a marvelous drive, in two small automobiles, one of which seated only two people and looked like a bullet. Uncle, Vera Arturovna, and I rode in the other car . . . I look a bit silly next to Vera Arturovna who is a tall beauty." On June 2, Tanya wrote that "Uncle took me, Vera Arturovna, and Ira [Belline] to the ballet. The whole theater looks at them."

80 L. to r., Sam Bottenheim, Respighi, Willem Mengelberg, Stravinsky, Rudolf Mengelberg, Alma Moodie, Staal (husband of Vera Janacopulos), Vera Janacopulos, Arthur Lourié. During this visit to Amsterdam, Stravinsky conducted *Le Sacre du printemps* for the first time.

81 *Summer 1926*. In the Hautes-Pyrénées, on an automobile trip between Paris and Monte Carlo. Photograph by Igor.

82

84

83

82, 83 *Paris 1926.*

84 *March 1926.* Vienna. Photo by Vera. "At first glance," Stravinsky's niece Tanya had written to her parents, "one gets the impression of a haughty and quite inaccessible character." On this concert trip to the Austrian capital, Stravinsky spent an afternoon with, among other musicians, Alban Berg and Anton Webern.

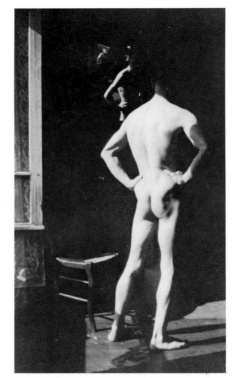

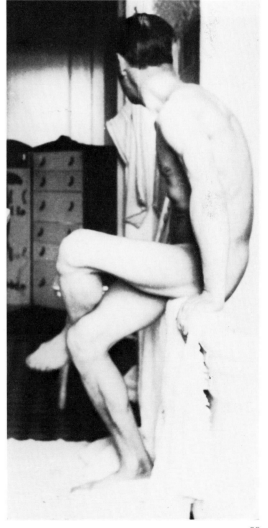

85 *July 1912.* Ustilug, Russia. During a heat-wave. Stravinsky seems to have sent copies of this photograph to Maurice Delage and Florent Schmitt.

86 *1923.* Château-Thierry. Stravinsky was proud of his muscle tone—he did daily gymnastics—but perhaps this is not the full explanation for his having preserved photographs of himself in the buff.

87 *Summer 1925.* Near Le Lavandou. Photo by Vera. On April 19, 1925, Tanya wrote to her parents: "Uncle is unbelievably lively, just exuding energy." She wrote again on May 14: "Uncle has returned from Toulon. You cannot imagine how phenomenally active he is. He takes very good care of himself and is so well-developed physically that he is just covered with muscles. He is extremely strong and can lift one-and-a-half times his weight with a single arm." On June 29, Tanya wrote home: "Physically Uncle is terribly strong and developed like an athlete; I want to move to Paris as soon as possible. . . . I would see more of Uncle than I do here."

88 *1930.* Berlin.

89

90

91

92

89, 90 *July 1926*. Paris. Le Bourget. Stravinsky, a wealthy friend Guy de Matharel, and Vera (above right), before flying to London.

91 *1927*. Paris. Le Bourget airport. L. to r., Michel Larionov, Paul Picasso, Serge Lifar, Walter Nouvel, and Pablo Picasso. Photo by Vera. Igor and Vera were invited to Paul Picasso's first communion, April 28, 1932 (Church of St. Augustine, Paris).

92 *April 25, 1931*. Trieste. Igor and Vera were about to take this seaplane to Venice. Stravinsky was fond of flying and never had any fear in airplanes, no matter how poor the weather conditions. (On May 11, 1935, Stravinsky's wife wrote to him in Copenhagen: ''I thank God that you had such a good flight, but I fear that this will give you the desire to fly more often instead of taking the train.'')

93 *July 1934*. Vera leaving Paris for London. Photograph by Igor.

93

94 *1927.* In Vera's apartment, 22, rue du Ranelagh. Photograph by Arthur Lourié, Stravinsky's musical assistant from 1924 to 1935. Stravinsky completed the orchestral score of *Oedipus Rex* in this room, May 11, 1927.

95

96

72

97

98

99

95 *1928*. Amsterdam. With the composer Albert Roussel. Photograph by Vera.

96 *January 1928*. Berlin. With Gavril Gavrilovich Païchadze, a close friend. Stravinsky was in the German capital to see his *Oedipus Rex* performed at the Kroll Oper.

97 Stravinsky dedicated *Apollo* to Vera, just as, five years earlier, he had dedicated the Octet to her: "Here is this Apollo, known as the leader of the Muses, which is to say, that which comes from Igor's true [vera] Muse, Vera."

98 *End of summer 1928*. Street in Scheveningen. "Concert tour with this miserable Schneevoigt," Stravinsky wrote under the photo (by Vera).

99 *1929*. Stravinsky's drawing of Erik Satie, after the bust and photographs of Satie made in 1925 by Robert Gaby. Gaby wrote to Stravinsky on April 19, 1929: "You were one of the first, perhaps *the* first – by the prestige of your authority – to draw attention to the essentially 'pure-music' quality of the music of Erik Satie . . . Allow me to repeat to you Satie's words a few days before his death. He told me, speaking of you, '*What a great man!* For Stravinsky the *question never arises* since it does not exist (the question of making concessions . . .). At the premiere of *Parade*, what made me tremble in my britches was the thought of my little *Parade* after *Petrushka*.'"

100 *1929*. Paris. Photo by Lipnitzki.

100

73

101

102

*Igor Strawinsky
Berlin
15 vi 1929*

103

104

105

101 *Summer 1929*. Echarvines, Haute-Savoie. With Serge Prokofiev and Ernest Ansermet.

102 *Summer 1929*. Vallée de Chevreuse.

103 *June 15, 1929*. Berlin. June 1929 was a very full month even by Stravinsky's standards. On June 1, he attended a concert in Paris conducted by Monteux and consisting of the *Firebird* Suite, the complete *Petrushka* and *Sacre du printemps*. On the 13th, he played his Concerto in Queen's Hall, London, at a matinee concert conducted by Eugene Goossens. The next day Igor and Vera were in Berlin, where a Richard Strauss festival had just ended. (Strauss accompanied a singer at the piano in five new songs, and conducted *Elektra*, *Intermezzo*, *Die Frau ohne Schatten*, and *Die Aegyptische Helene*.) On June 17, Stravinsky played his Concerto in the Staatsoper in a concert conducted by Otto Klemperer that began with *Apollo* and ended with *Les Noces* (in which the first and second piano parts were played by Fritz Zweig and George Szell, and for which the chorus was prepared by Schoenberg's pupil Karl Rankl). On June 20 and 21, the Diaghilev Ballet presented *Apollo* and *Le Sacre* in Charlottenburg, but Stravinsky returned to Paris without seeing any of the performances. He was in London again for a concert on June 27.

104 *January 30, 1930*. Leipzig. A few weeks earlier, Stravinsky had begun to compose the *Symphony of Psalms*. Just before the premiere of the new work, at the end of the year, he gave an interview in Mannheim, where he had a concert on December 9: "My title is *Symphonie de Psaumes*, not *Symphonie psalmique*, for the latter would describe the style, while the former designates the content. The Psalms of David are the foundations for the work. The chorus is used, not for a final effect, as in Beethoven's Ninth Symphony, but throughout. The composition is in three parts: first movement—prelude; second movement—double fugue; third movement—allegro sinfonica . . . The last movement represents the classical symphonic form itself, and, in the language of form-theory, it is a sonata movement. The symphonic form is seen in a new perspective . . ." (*Neue Badische Landes-Zeitung*, December 8, 1930)

105 *1930*. Rose Hotel, Wiesbaden.

106

107

108

109

110

106 *February 17, 1930.* Bucharest to Prague. Photo by Stravinsky. In Prague, on February 21, Stravinsky gave an interview to the Prager Presse in which quarter-tone music, Mahler, and the as-yet-unnamed *Symphony of Psalms* were discussed. (In spite of his disparagement of quarter-tone music, Stravinsky dined with Alois Haba during the visit to the Czech city.) In this same interview, Stravinsky denied that anything "Russian" could be heard in his music anymore, and asked his interviewers if they could detect any Russian element in his *Oedipus Rex*.

In May 1930, Igor and Vera were in Brussels, where he conducted a concert on the 22nd (*Pulcinella* Suite, *Song of the Nightingale*, *Le Baiser de la fée*), then in Amsterdam, where on the 28th he led the Octet, *Mavra*, and a staged performance of *Histoire du soldat*.

107 *February 17, 1930.* Bucharest to Prague. Igor and Vera went to Romania following a concert in Düsseldorf on February 6 (in which he had conducted *Apollo*, the Two Little Suites, the *Petrushka* Suite and the *Firebird* Suite). In Bucharest he played the Capriccio on February 12 and on the 16th conducted a program of the Symphony in E flat, *Fireworks*, Scherzo fantastique, and *Petrushka* Suite.

108 *January 22, 1930.* Staatstheater Berlin. On this date Klemperer conducted *Le Baiser de la fée*, Mozart's G Minor Symphony, and Stravinsky's Capriccio with the composer as soloist. On January 30, in the Gewandhaus (Leipzig), Klemperer again conducted the Capriccio with Stravinsky as soloist, this time on a program with the First Symphony of Brahms and the Chaconne from Gluck's *Orpheus*.

"I don't like conductors," Stravinsky said, "and all conductors hate me. [Otto Klemperer was an exception.] They respect me, but they hate me. This is because they cannot play my music correctly . . . Conductors are more interested in expressing themselves than the music before them. My music will not take 'glamour;' it must speak for itself . . ." (*The Houston Post*, January 26, 1949).

109 *November 12, 1930.* Munich. Photo by Eric Schall.

110 *October 24, 1930.* Mainz. The period from early October through mid-December 1930 was one of Stravinsky's most active as a performing artist. He gave concerts in Zürich, Lausanne, Geneva, Mainz (on October 25), Wiesbaden, Bremen, Berlin, Munich, Frankfurt, Nuremberg, Mannheim, Brussels, Amsterdam and Paris.

111

111 *November 1930*. Vienna. After playing the Capriccio in a concert.

112 *April 29, 1931*. At Gardone and Verona. On April 9, 1931, Igor and Vera left Genoa for Trieste, where they arrived at 7 a.m. on the 20th (Savoia Excelsior Palace Hotel). On the 24th, in the "Teatro Communale G. Verdi," Stravinsky conducted a concert of excerpts from *Le Baiser de la fée* (Prologue, Village Festival, At the Mill, Berceuse), the Two Little Suites, and the *Pulcinella* and *Firebird* Suites. One of his hosts in Trieste was Rhené Baton, director of the orchestra there and the second conductor ever to lead the *Sacre du printemps* (in London in July 1913). Another host was Giovanni Sbisa (a concert agent), and another Mario Nordio, editor of *Il Piccolo di Trieste*, to which Stravinsky gave one of his most important interviews. On the 25th, Igor and Vera went to Venice in a seaplane, whose "*pilota aviatore*," Paolo Cosulich, presented his two passengers with an autographed calling card. In Venice, they stayed in the Hotel Bauer Grünwald. On the 27th, after a visit to the Museo Correr, they left for Padua (Grand Hotel Storione), and on the 28th they stayed in the Hotel Colomba D'Oro, Verona. The following day they stopped at Lago di Garda.

113 *April 1931*. Lago di Garda.

114 *1931*. Florence.

115

116

115 *November 18, 1931.* Ostend to Dover.

116 *November 1931.* Wiesbaden.

117 *November 23, 1931.* Wiesbaden. Vera and
Igor had just returned from London, where he
conducted the Violin Concerto and *Symphony
of Psalms.* Back in Germany, they attended a
performance of *La Forza del Destino* on
November 22. In Cologne, on December 1, he
conducted the Violin Concerto and played his
Capriccio, and in Hanover, on the 14th, he
and Samuel Dushkin performed the Violin
Concerto. The next day, Igor and Vera were
in Paris in the Salle Gaveau listening to a
concert that included Schoenberg's
orchestrations of two Bach chorale preludes,
Satie's *Parade,* and the *Sacre.* Raïssa Maritain
wrote in her Journal: "Curious performance:
everyone is there: Stravinsky, Lourié,
Nabokov, Markevitch, Bérard . . . Cocteau,
Julien Green, Max Jacob . . . Le Sacre seems
to me more beautiful every time I hear it . . .
We see Stravinsky after the concert . . ."

118 *December 9, 1931.* Wiesbaden.

117

118

119

120

119, 120, 122, 123 *March 17, 1932*. Venice, on the Lido (opposite), on a bridge, and with the Tetrarch (corner of the Cathedral of St. Mark). Photographs by Vera and Igor, who arrived in the city (Hotel Bauer Grünwald) on March 16. They had come from Belgium where, on the 14th, he had played the Capriccio in Antwerp, and, on the 15th, attended a concert in Brussels that included his 1906 Symphony and *The Faun and the Shepherdess*. On the 19th, in the Teatro La Fenice, he conducted a concert that consisted of the 1st, 2nd, and 4th tableaux of *Petrushka*, the two Little Suites, the Scherzo Fantastique, and *Firebird* Suite.

121 *March 1932*. Venice. In front of the Teatro La Fenice.

124, 125 *March 1932*. Venice. Photos by Vera and Igor.

82

121

124

122

123

125

126 [Home, to Grünwald
     To the quiet and my bed.
     What a life, what a hotel!
     But there . . . I've my chess.]

Quatrain written by Igor in Vera's diary.

127, 128, 129 *March 20, 1932*. San Michele.
Bringing flowers to Diaghilev's grave. Photo
of the grave by Igor. In an inspired, if also
calculated, act of matchmaking, the impresario
had introduced Igor and Vera in February
1921. Among the letters of condolence that
Stravinsky received when Diaghilev died,
only one, from Vera, expresses sympathy for
all of Diaghilev's friends, nor does any letter
state more poignantly the sense of loss that all
those who loved Diaghilev and the Ballets
Russes must have felt:

"The death of Diaghilev has shaken me
terribly. I have not been able to pull myself
together since this morning, and I can think of
nothing else. I am distraught and sad. I sent
you a telegram thinking that you might not
have heard. I learned about it from the
newspapers. Then Argutinsky telephoned. He
didn't know any of the details, but he gave me
the address of Pavka'[Diaghilev's uncle], to
whom I sent a telegram (Koribut, Grand Hôtel
des Bains, Venice). Lately Pavka has been
receiving the most tender letters from
Diaghilev, more tender than ever before. On
Saturday, Diaghilev, feeling very ill, sent for
him. According to the newspapers, death is
attributed to blood poisoning. Pavka sent a
telegram to Argutinsky saying that Diaghilev
had died *sans souffrance*. All of his friends are
there now, Misia, Chanel, and others, so he
was not alone among the young, who
probably lost their heads.

"My friendship with you is linked to my
friendship with Diaghilev. I cannot separate
our relationship from that period. All morning
I cried and cried.

"What will happen to the whole Russian
Ballet now? Does this mean that everything is
finished—all of the Russian season? Will there
be no more performances? I feel sorry for the
old fellows, Valechka [Walter Nouvel,
Diaghilev's oldest friend], Pavka—who will
now be thrown out onto the street. All this is
terribly sad . . ."

130 *March 20, 1932*. San Michele. Photo by
Vera. 29 years later, Stravinsky's own funeral
procession was to pass the place where he is
standing.

126

127

128

129

130

131

131 *June 1932.* En route to Dijon. Photo by Igor. He spent his 50th birthday with his family in Voreppe, joining Vera the next day. On June 2 in Frankfurt, they heard a performance of *Mavra* conducted by Hans Rosbaud. On the 24th they dined with the Streckers in Wiesbaden, on the 26th they were in Heidelberg, and on the 27th at the Maison Rouge in Strasbourg. At the beginning of July, Igor and Vera attended Arthur Rubinstein's wedding in Paris. Back in Voreppe, Stravinsky completed the Duo concertant and received visits, at the beginning of August, from Arthur Lourié and Samuel Dushkin.

132 In mid-August 1932, Igor and Vera drove to Biarritz, by way of Tarascon, Aigues-Mortes, Arles (17–19, Hôtel Jules César), Les Baux (20th), Carcassonne, arriving at the Hôtel du Palais, Biarritz, on the 21st. During the next two days, Stravinsky rehearsed the Casino orchestra for a concert on the ·25th. Igor and Vera spent part of that day at the country home of a friend, the Marquis Lur-Saluce (Château Yquem) in Gavarny (below). On September 1 and 2, Igor and Vera returned to Paris with their friends, M. and Mme Blaise Cendrars (left, at a luncheon in Bordeaux for Cendrars' 45th birthday). The foursome stopped in Bordeaux (Château Montre), St. Emilion, Château-Biron, Périgueux, Eglise de Dorat, Limoges (Château de Jouxtens – L'Albi Jouxtens wrote to Stravinsky October 9, 1933, asking whether a musical son ''should go to the Juilliard School in New York?''), Poitiers (Hôtel du Palais), Chalon-sur-Saône (Grand Hôtel Moderne). After spending the night of September 2 at Chartres (Hôtel de France), the party reached Paris on the 3rd.

132

133 *August 26, 1932.* Gavarny, near Biarritz. With the Marquis Lur-Saluce.

133

134

134 *1932*. Locarno.

135 *End of October 1932*. Berlin.

136 *February 3, 1933*. On a streetcar in
Munich. Stravinsky had played his Capriccio
in Hamburg on January 23 and in Ostrava on
January 26 (on a program with Jaroslav Vogel
conducting the *Symphony of Psalms* and the
Pulcinella and *Petrushka* suites). The
composer (Passport No. 20508, delivered by
the Prefect of Police, Paris, May 15, 1930) had
stipulated with his Czechoslovak concert
agency that he and Mme Sudeikina should not
be wakened when their train from Germany
crossed the border during the night. The day
after the concert (and post-concert dinner at
Oskar Federer's), Vera and Igor went to
Wiesbaden. Samuel Dushkin joined them
there and, on February 1, went with them by
train to Munich (Bayerische Hof) where the
composer and the violinist gave a recital in
the Odeon Theater on February 2. Thomas
Mann greeted Stravinsky backstage
afterwards and invited him to dine at the
Mann home. On February 6, Igor and Vera
went to Milan, and on February 11, the Manns
fled to Holland. The Stravinskys and Manns
next saw each other in the early 1940s in
Hollywood.

137

138

A Turin avec Rota, Virardi Paoli

139

137, 138 *1933.* Milan and Turin. Nino Rota, the future composer of almost all the music for Fellini's films, was only twenty-one when these photographs were taken. He had just returned from a year of study at the Curtis Institute of Music in Philadelphia. Rota was constantly in Stravinsky's company during his Italian tours of 1933 and 1934 (Venice). After hearing the BBC broadcast of *Perséphone* in November 1934, Rota wrote to the composer: "I hope that for the next performances you can find a less monotonous and disagreeable voice than that of Mme Ida Rubinstein." The scene above left of mannequins in a shop window seems to anticipate one of the Fellini movies that made Rota (d. 1979) famous.

Domenico De' Paoli published an important monograph on Stravinsky (1931), visited him in Paris, Voreppe, London, and continued to write about him until the 1950s.

139 *February 12, 1933.* Turin. Stravinsky conducted a concert in Milan on February 11 and another one in Turin (*Petrushka* and *Firebird* Suites, *Fireworks*, *Symphony of Psalms*) on the 17th. On the 18th he and Vera went to Rome (Hotel Excelsior) for a concert on the 22nd.

On the lit el-le re-po-se Et je n'ose la troubler

140

140 In memory of a summer of oppressive
   summer weeks
 When my dear Persephone
 Behind a shutter seeking cool and calm
 Hiding from a crowd of friends and humidity
 From the unavoidable, that she cannot
   hide from, rings of the phone—
 From morning on for the whole day
   snuggled in bed.
   I. Stravinsky, Voreppe, August 1933.

141 Vera was present at Igor's meetings with
André Gide—in Wiesbaden at the end of
January 1933—to plan the scenario of
Perséphone. Two months later, Païchadze
wrote to Stravinsky: ''I am forwarding a letter
from Gide which evidently contains some of
the Priest's [Eumolpus'] poetry . . . I gave
Vera Arturovna a brief account of my
conversation with Gide and Ida Rubinstein.
Now I await your return to Paris to discuss
with you the final deadline arrangements for
the work, after which I will sign the contract.''
(March 27, 1933)

142 *April 1933*. Budapest. Photograph from a newspaper. Reporters followed Stravinsky closely during his sojourn in the Hungarian capital (Carlton Hotel, March 27–April 4), and he and Vera were photographed sitting in cafés and gazing at the Beethoven plaque ("Stravinsky meets Beethoven"). Stravinsky had been invited to Budapest to conduct a "Composers' Soirée" in which the soloist in his Concerto was Rosalinda Kaplan, a 14-year-old prodigy from Chicago. After the concert (April 3), Stravinsky wrote to her manager: "She has the most excellent pianistic qualities, but also a gift of understanding and assimilating ideas." The following description of Stravinsky in Budapest is from the newspaper *Magyarsag*: "The artist who yesterday attracted much attention in his maroon shirt, today appeared in a dark blue

one . . . He went to King Mathias Church where he crossed himself in the Russian manner in front of each altar. He asked for the sexton and inquired where candles could be bought. Soon some candles were found. Stravinsky placed them in front of the altar and prayed for a long time." Hardly a newspaper report about Stravinsky throughout his life fails to mention his clothes. And not only newspapers. His niece Tanya wrote home on April 19, 1925: "How smartly he dresses (silk handkerchief, monocle, knitted jackets of various colors which he changes almost every day)." Three weeks later she wrote, "He dresses stunningly and has a vast number of neckties."

143 *Summer 1933*. Combloux. During the composition of *Perséphone*.

146

144 *November 20, 1933*. Rome.

145 *March 1935*. Boston. With Arthur Fiedler, after a rehearsal of *Perséphone*, for which Fiedler prepared the chorus.

146 *May 22, 1935*. Bologna. On the day after this picture was taken, Stravinsky conducted a concert in the Teatro Duse. In addition to three of his own works, the program included the *Nutcracker* Suite and Glinka's *Ruslan* Overture and *Kamarinskaya*. Igor and Vera had come to Bologna from Venice, as they had done in September of the year before. On this second visit, they stayed in the Majestic Hotel, where, on May 21, a telegram arrived from Ida Rubinstein cancelling her engagement to appear the following week with Stravinsky in Rome in *Perséphone*. Stravinsky and Vera stayed in the Excelsior Hotel, Rome, from the 24th to the 30th, and on the 30th, in the Augusteo, Stravinsky conducted a substitute program of the *Petrushka* and *Firebird* suites, Debussy's *Nuages* and *Fêtes*, and Dukas' *L'Apprenti sorcier*. On the afternoon of May 29, Mussolini received Stravinsky in the Palazzo Venezia.

147

147 *September 1937.* On the beach at Lago Maggiore.

148 *1936.* Vera in her Rue de l'Assomption apartment.

149 *March 1937.* New York. The Metropolitan Opera House. Rehearsal of *Jeu de cartes.* Nicolas Kopeikin, Diaghilev's rehearsal pianist who came to New York in 1933 to work for Balanchine (far right) and the banker Gerald Warburg are looking at Stravinsky. Dushkin is seated next to Stravinsky, Balanchine at the end of the row. The tall figure facing the piano is Lincoln Kirstein.

150 *March 1937.* New York.

151 *March 1937.* With Charles Chaplin at his home.

152 *April 1937.* New York, the Sulgrave Hotel. Photographed by Fritz Reiner. Twenty years later, on Stravinsky's seventy-fifth birthday, Reiner sent the following telegram: "*Laudate eum in cymbalis bene sonantibus laudate eum in cymbalis jubilationibus alleluia cliens devotissimus fidelis. Fredericus Reiner.*"

148

149

150

151

152

153 *December 1939*. Hollywood. With Walt
Disney and George Balanchine.

154 *1939*. Paris. Photograph by Hoyningen-
Huené. On August 28, 1939, Willy Strecker,
the music publisher (B. Schotts Söhne, Mainz),
wrote to Stravinsky: "What will always be the
leitmotif of my visit is Frau Vera's radiance
and warmth."

154

153

155

155 *March 9, 1940.* Bedford, Massachusetts. On their wedding day.

156 *March 17, 1940.* Boston. With Alexis Kall. Vera's diary for this date reads: "Lunch at Forbes. At 3 we drive to Back Bay Station to fetch Adele Marcus, then to Exeter for Kall's lecture and the Concerto for Two Pianos." (Actually, Stravinsky read a lecture, not Kall.) On March 1, Vera had written in her diary: "I arrive in Boston from Charleston at midnight, and Igor brings me to the house of Edward Forbes; I am glad to be in a civilized home." On March 4 she wrote: "It is a nice life in this country house. Squirrels take nuts from your hands, and dogs run in the snow." In the Forbes home, in February 1949, the composer met Dr. Max Rinkel (d. 1966), the pioneer researcher in lysergic acid diethylamide, who, with Dr. Jules Pierre and Dr. David Protetch of New York, became one of the composer's East Coast physicians in the 1950s.

Dr. Alexis Fyodorovich Kall, philologist, was a classmate of Stravinsky's at the University of St. Petersburg and became his secretary in the U.S. from September 1939. He translated for Stravinsky during his composition teaching at Harvard.

156

From *The Boston Daily Globe*. March 25, 1940.

RUSSIAN COMPOSER, BRIDE, HONEYMOONING IN BOSTON

When Igor Stravinsky lifts his baton to conduct the Boston Symphony Orchestra in his *Oedipus Rex* and *Apollo* next Friday and Saturday, he will do so with a flourish that his audiences have not seen for more than a year now. Not that the noted Russian composer is feeling particularly well physically. "*Mais non*," he does not like this winter weather—he has a cold in the head—and it gives him headaches. But he is happier than he has been in a long time. For two weeks now the diminutive, moody master musician has been happy. His usually serious expression is often transformed by a "catching" smile. He looks young for his 57 years, despite the gray mustache and sparse gray hair. He talks animatedly to his friends in fluent, sparkling French. He is like a man in love. He is a man in love.

Stravinsky and his bride of two weeks, to whom he was married at the home of friends, Dr. and Mrs. T. A. Taracouzio, in Bedford, have been honeymooning at Hotel Hemenway, Back Bay. The former Vera de Bosset is a very attractive, tall brunette. She is very good for Stravinsky—because she is of such a gay nature. Her dark eyes sparkle and her pretty mouth is always curling at the corners . . . [When] Stravinsky came here in October, at the invitation of Harvard, to be Charles Eliot Norton lecturer in poetry, he was not happy separated from the woman who was to become his wife, even though they corresponded frequently. So Vera de Bosset Sudeikina came to this country for the first time last January.

Stravinsky met the liner *Rex*, which brought her to New York, but the pair eluded photographers and newspapermen. Until plans for their wedding could be completed, Vera went to visit with friends in Charleston, South Carolina, while Stravinsky returned to his work at Harvard. The wedding was a simple, civil ceremony by Justice of the Peace Arthur Carson performed in Bedford on March 9. Now the couple would like to make their home in the United States, preferably in Los Angeles, and they will stay in this country as long as their leave can be extended.

Next week he will go to New York to conduct the Philharmonic Orchestra and in May the Stravinskys will journey to Los

157

158

Angeles, there to make their home during the remainder of their stay in this country.

Yesterday the Stravinskys posed in their suite at the Hotel Hemenway for the first pictures which have been taken since their wedding. They were also the first photographs made of Mrs. Stravinsky in this country. The honeymooners were cheerful and happy, despite Stravinsky's cold and aching head. . . .

157 *April 1940.* Boston, Back Bay Station. During the first seven months of 1940, Stravinsky married; completed the third movement of his Symphony in C; read three lectures at Harvard and taught students there; went to Washington to obtain permission for himself and his wife to remain in the United States; conducted a total of eighteen concerts with the New York Philharmonic, the Pittsburgh, Chicago, and Boston Symphony Orchestras; conducted several recording sessions with the New York Philharmonic; participated in chamber-music concerts, both as pianist and conductor, in Boston, New York, and other cities; moved from Boston to California (boat to New York, another boat to Miami and Galveston, then by train); rented a house in Beverly Hills; composed the last movement of the Symphony; and conducted concerts in Mexico.

158 *July 1940.* Taxco. Photograph by Vera.

159 *July 1940.* Guadalajara.

161 *August 9, 1940.* Los Angeles, Union Station. The Stravinskys re-entered the United States from Mexico on August 8, as Russian non-preference quota immigrants. The next day in Los Angeles, they were greeted by Adolph Bolm, and the day after, they received their first papers for United States citizenship.

162 *September 1940.* At 124 South Swall Drive, Beverly Hills, the Stravinskys' home from May 23 to November 1, 1940. On August 27, in Hollywood Bowl, Stravinsky conducted *Firebird*, Tchaikovsky's Second Symphony and the *Nutcracker* Suite. From September 6 to 13, the Stravinskys and Bolms drove to Carmel, San Francisco, Yosemite. In late September and October, Stravinsky composed the Tango, made an arrangement of the Star-Spangled Banner, and began an arrangement of a purely instrumental version of *Renard*.

159

Double take. Igor Stravinsky, Russian-born composer, and his wife are happy because they've just been naturalized in Los Angeles.

160

BACK FROM MEXICO—Composer Igor Stravinsky, left, accompanied by Mrs. Stravinsky, is shown as they were greeted by Adolph Bolm, at the train on which they returned from Mexico City. Stravinsky will conduct his "Firebird" Tuesday in Hollywood Bowl for Bolm's Ballet.

161

162

163 *Thanksgiving 1940*. Cincinnati, at the home of Lucien Wulsin, president of Baldwin Piano Company and a long-time friend of the composer. Photograph by Eugene Goossens. On November 2, after having given up their rented house in Beverly Hills and placing their possessions in storage, the Stravinskys left by train for Chicago, where they stayed at the home of John Alden Carpenter, a friend since 1925. On November 7, Stravinsky conducted the Chicago Symphony in the world premiere of his Symphony in C, the first of three performances there. From November 17 to 24, the Stravinskys were in Cincinnati as Wulsin's house guests. On November 22, and again the following night, Stravinsky conducted the Cincinnati Symphony Orchestra in *Jeu de cartes*, the Symphony in C and *Le Sacre du printemps*. On the 26th, the Stravinskys were in New York, at the Barbizon Plaza. Vera Stravinsky's diary for November 29 reads: "Igor is moody. Lunch at Longchamps, then to Cartier where we see [Vladimir] Dukelsky. Igor dislikes him. At 5, Alice Nikitina for tea. Igor plays Bach." On December 20, the Stravinskys went to Minneapolis, where he conducted a concert. Then, back in New York, in the lobby of the Barbizon, Mrs. Stravinsky received a visit from Serge Sudeikin, their first and last meeting since 1922. Sudeikin married the American singer Jean Palmer. He died in 1946 and was buried in Woodstock, New York.

163

164 *January 6, 1941*. Washington, D.C. According to the *Times-Herald*, "Igor Stravinsky, most celebrated of Russian composers, guest conductor with the National Symphony tomorrow in a program of his own music and the music of Tchaikovsky, surprised his interviewers yesterday with two announcements: He has applied for his first citizenship papers; he has acquired a second wife . . . who . . . spoke only to help her husband with an occasional English word. She is a handsome woman and was a smiling and gracious hostess to the press as we gathered in the dressing room after rehearsal. Stravinsky talked freely of his contemporaries in the field of composition. 'Schoenberg,' he explained, commenting on the recent riot [premiere of the Violin Concerto] of the dowagers at the Philadelphia Orchestra concert under Stokowski, 'Schoenberg is a strong man, a clever man . . . I dislike the music of Scriabin, and the music of Rimsky-Korsakov, though I studied with him. I want my music to be simple, relatively free from dissonance . . .' Asked the inevitable question [about] swing, he implied that its present values are slight."

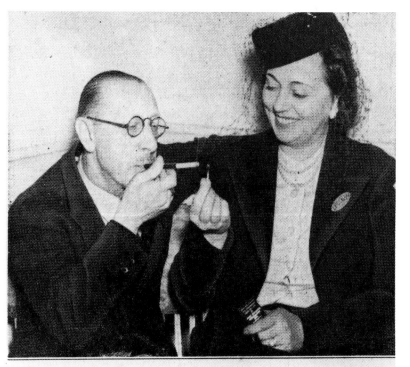

Times-Herald Photo

Noted Russian Composer Brings Bride to Washington

Igor Stravinsky, who will conduct the National Symphony Orchestra tomorrow evening, is shown here with his second wife, the former Vera Dosset, during the composer's press interview here yesterday before rehearsing with the orchestra at Constitution Hall.

164

165

166

167

165 *January 22, 1941*. New York. The Fifty-First Street Theater (which was only partly heated). With Balanchine, at the dress rehearsal of *Balustrade*.

166, 167 *July 1941*. Mexico.

169

168

168 *February 1942*. The Hotel Whitcomb, San Francisco. Photograph from *San Francisco Life*.

169 *1942*. Santa Barbara.

170 *Hollywood, June 18, 1942*. Stravinsky's sixtieth birthday. Photograph by Man Ray.

171, 172, 173 *Summer 1944*. Santa Barbara.

170

171

172

173

174 *September 8, 1945.* Vera at home. Photograph by *Life* Magazine.

175 *1946.* 1260 North Wetherly Drive. Both Igor and Vera lived in this house longer than in any other in their entire lives. John Malcolm Brinnin has described the Stravinskys in their home, during a visit with Henri Cartier-Bresson, May 27, 1947: ''The room Stravinsky uses as a studio has the point-device economy and efficient elegance of a ship's bridge. One sheet of music, a masterpiece of calligraphy from his own hand, has been placed above the keyboard . . . On a bone-white wall hangs one framed drawing: a head of Beethoven as a young man. Under its massive, self-possessed stare Stravinsky's movements seem light as an acrobat's. Without being asked to, he places himself in half a dozen likely photographic settings. 'This you must see,' he says, and whisks from his desk a newspaper clipping, an account of the arrest by government agents, for tax evasion, of one Dr. Petrouchka. 'It comes in the post,' he says, 'No name, nothing . . .'

''We join Mme Stravinsky, whose name is Vera, for coffee in a drawing room dominated by a cage of white birds. Considerably larger in girth and stature than her husband, whom she calls Eager, she pours from a silver coffeepot and presides in the manner of someone honoring a familiar ritual. 'Our neighbor, Oona Chaplin, has found this terrific *boulanger*,' she says, and holds out a plate of powdered digits. As she and Cartier begin to reminisce in French, Stravinsky taps my knee. 'Come,' he says, 'we shall visit the garden.' We step onto a terrace above which is another terrace with trellises and an orange tree. 'On days [when] I wonder who I am,' he says, 'I climb to see the ocean. One look, then I climb down . . . You lift yourself to the branch, you look away from the sun, you see, like a floor maybe, one piece of blue.'

''When it's time to leave, he walks me to the car while Henri and Mme Stravinsky follow behind. 'You must not be so much the journalist,' he says. 'A journalist must hurry and do much, he must always *use* things. The poet, he has only to *be*, and to wait. Patience. You have lived with this man Cartier-Bresson, I know already you have much patience.' ''

176 *1944.* 1260 North Wetherly Drive. With George Balanchine.

175

177 *1946*. Igor photographed by Vera from the street, 1260 North Wetherly Drive.

178 *1946*. Vera photographed by Igor from the front lawn of their home. The bedroom has flowers on the windowsill.

178

179 *October 1945.* In "La Boutique," the art gallery on La Cienega Boulevard, Hollywood, founded in August 1945 by Vera and her friend Lisa Sokolov (see p. 104). They gave exhibitions of pre-Columbian sculpture, of Picasso, Klee, Chagall, Dali, Tchelichev, Eugene Berman, as well as of Vera's own creations of bouquets of flowers made of rice paper; of bouquets made of old fabrics and beads placed in tiny vases; of stones painted and decorated with sequins; of dried sponges; of iridescent butterflies in glass boxes. In October and November 1945, Vera's "Madonnas," collages made of fabrics, jewels, beads, sequins, and other materials, were exhibited at the Pasadena Art Institute. The *Pasadena Star-News and Post*, October 23, 1945, quoted her: "One day in early autumn, in central France, I went . . . to a village. The people were bringing back the statue of the Madonna from the mountains, where she had been taken to protect the cattle during the summer. The people changed all of her clothes, and dressed her in lace, embroidery, jewels, and a crown . . . About ten o'clock at night the procession came down from the mountain. In the church everyone paid homage to the beautiful Madonna, some of the people dancing, others playing music."

180 *1946.* 1260 North Wetherly Drive. Giving a Russian lesson to Benny Goodman.

181 *January 1947.* San Antonio. Besides conducting the San Antonio Symphony Orchestra, Stravinsky led a rehearsal of the Army Air Force Band at Randolph Field. Here he is photographed with earphones at a recording lathe. On January 24, the *San Antonio Evening News* published a photograph of the door of the St. Anthony Hotel's room 584 and its sign "DO NOT DISTURB." The newspaper reported that a woman dressed in a housecoat peered into the hallway, said "Ooooooh! What's this? What is it that you want?", was told that the newsman waiting in the corridor wanted to interview Igor Stravinsky, answered, "Oh, but now you cannot do this. Mr. Stravinsky wants to rest today. Everybody comes back tomorrow at A.M." Mrs. Stravinsky closed the door. The interview ended.

179

180

181

182

succès, triomphe au Roi David, mon cher Milhaud

183

184

182, 183 *August 1947*. San Pedro, California. Photograph by Madeleine Milhaud. Darius Milhaud (in the wheelchair), about to embark on a steamer for France, via the Panama Canal, is being seen off by, l. to r., Germain Prévost (violist and a friend of Stravinsky's since the 1920s), Eve Babitz (the child, future writer), and Mrs. Sol Babitz, Vladimir Sokolov (the actor), the Stravinskys, Mrs. Sokolov. In a letter to Stravinsky for his 75th birthday, Milhaud said that he was proud to have been present at the first performance of the *Firebird* (June 25, 1910). Stravinsky sent the "12-tone" greeting to Milhaud on the occasion of the La Scala premiere of his opera *David*.

184 *1948*. California.

185

186

187

185 *1947*. 1260 North Wetherly Drive.

186 *1950*. 1260 North Wetherly Drive.

187 *January 25, 1949*. Houston. On January 31, 1949, Stravinsky conducted the Houston Symphony Orchestra. The following interview by Hubert Roussel appeared in the *Houston Post*, January 26:

"HOUSTON JINX LETS UP ON STRAVINSKY—
NOT A MOMENT TOO SOON: Houston may be remembered in history in that it derailed the honeymoon of the greatest composer of the twentieth century. That happened in 1940 . . . and when Igor Stravinsky returned Tuesday, again with his wife, the jinx apparently met him at the station. There was a mixup in his understanding with the Rice Hotel, and the suite he had ordered turned out to be a single room in which he didn't dare open his 10 pieces of luggage for fear of walling himself up in a corner. All day he and Mrs. Stravinsky sat glumly and waited. The weather reminded them of California, which is home, and they were sad and depressed. But at 6 p.m. the fates finally relented, and the man who has exerted the most profoundly pervasive influence on modern music was moved to a suite. He now felt he could stretch his legs—which *he* could do in a telephone booth—and, being obviously an individual of mercurial nature, he was suddenly happy and jovial. He sat down with this reporter, the very first caller, and talked volubly about practically everything—including his other and heretofore unknown visit to Houston.

"The Russian-born master and the present Mrs. Stravinsky were married eight years ago. They set out from New York on a honeymoon trip to the Grand Canyon. The first stage of the journey was made by boat, which landed the couple in Galveston. They didn't like it. They hurried directly to Houston, took a look at the city—and gave up. 'It was a terrible trip in every way,' said Igor Stravinsky, waving a long cigarette holder. 'The boat was bad—very bad—and so was the ocean that year—and then at the end there was Galveston. We wanted to rest—but not there. We took the first train to Houston. We got off and looked around—and then got back on and went home. That honeymoon—it was a French debacle.'

"But Stravinsky bears no bitterness in his mellow and philosophical heart. At 66 he expects and appreciates life's ironies. Besides, he has learned to love Texas since—from visits to San Antonio, Dallas and Fort Worth, and now, back in Houston, he finds it isn't at all what he thought. 'This is a great, a wonderful city—more throbbing and alive than the others,' he said. 'You feel that. Like everything in Texas, it is big, fresh, vital. We should have looked farther than in front of the station in 1940—we didn't know.'"

188 *March 1949*. Palm Springs, with a surrey. Bonnie and Clyde.

189 *January 1957*. New York. Invitation and guest book at the Iolas Gallery's exhibition of Vera Stravinsky's paintings. Vera became a full-time painter in 1949, but she did not exhibit until 1955 (April 15, Galleria Obelisco, Rome). Nature—leaves, flowers, seashells, clouds—is the material of her painting, but she prefers nature in a certain mood, rainy rather than sunny. "I like the *mélancolie* in a landscape," she says, "and I like early morning mists, woods and fields blurred by rain, night scenes with mysterious explosions of light." Her first American pictures were inspired by automobile trips through Louisiana and the redwood forests of the Northwest. (The Stravinskys traveled extensively by automobile in their first two decades in the United States.) Oil rigs were another source of inspiration, "but at night, when they look like Christmas trees." She continued to paint in Europe, too, on each return there in the 1950s and 1960s, most rewardingly in Venice.

Yet her pictures are not really "of" any of these places or "of" any "thing." She does not copy and does not sketch, or even take notes except for verbal reminders of the colors in a composition of nature. To her, color *is* composition, and her greatest gifts are an infallible color sense and skill in color manipulation. "My imagination is ignited from the outside," she says, "but I paint from the inside, depending on imagination alone. I try to forget the relationship with the object when I begin to paint. Birds, fish, fragments of objects, *natures mortes*: they must retain no more than a *soupçon* of reality in the painting."

Vera is a gouache painter, first and foremost, partly because she likes the velvety texture. Her techniques are her own. She applies paint with any implement—spatula, sponge, palette, knife, sable brush, the flat of her hand. And she treats a painting by several different means, rubbing it with paper, scratching it with a table fork, even washing it in her bathtub. In the case of work that displeases her—and her touchstones tell her immediately—this washing is an act of purification, the need to begin with a clean slate. She will briefly immerse a gouache in the bath, and after the baptismal waters have dried, paint a new surface on the old.

On January 5, 1958, the following interview and article appeared in the *Houston Post*. "'I found it terribly dull to be only a housewife,' said Mrs. Igor Stravinsky, musingly . . . So, she turned to art. First she did collages—designs developed from pieces of paper and paste. Then, she turned to other mediums, wash, ink, oil.

"She has had shows in New York, Milan, at the Pasadena and Santa Barbara Art Museums, in Santa Fe, at the Los Angeles County Museum. She has had art critics talking happily, and what's more, she has sold, and well. Houstonians will be able to view some 20 of her pieces at a show at the Cushman Gallery, beginning Monday . . . 'I have always been afraid to have a teacher,' said the self-taught Mrs. Stravinsky. 'A teacher often has so much influence. When you take lessons, you begin painting like your teacher . . .' Mrs. Stravinsky, whose paintings are imaginative, individual treatments of such subjects as oilfields and Sunset Boulevard, says she likes best to paint night scenes, flowers, trees, water—'but not a man sitting in a cafe with a cigar. I look, look, and look again. I have no good memory of names, I never remember them, but those things I want to paint I remember exactly.' Mrs. Stravinsky [is] a handsome, quick-smiling woman of Russian birth and long-standing Parisian culture."

188

189

190

191

190 *August 1951.* Naples. Stravinsky's physician, Dr. Musella, is in the background.

191 *August 1951.* In front of 1260 North Wetherly Drive, leaving for the railroad station, New York, Naples and Venice.

192 *October 1951.* Baden-Baden. On a balcony at the Brenners Park Hotel.

193 *March 3, 1951.* Havana. Stravinsky conducted the following program with the Orquesta Filarmónica de La Habana on Sunday morning, March 4, and Monday evening, March 5: Octet, *Scènes de Ballet*, Eight Easy Pieces, Divertimento.

192

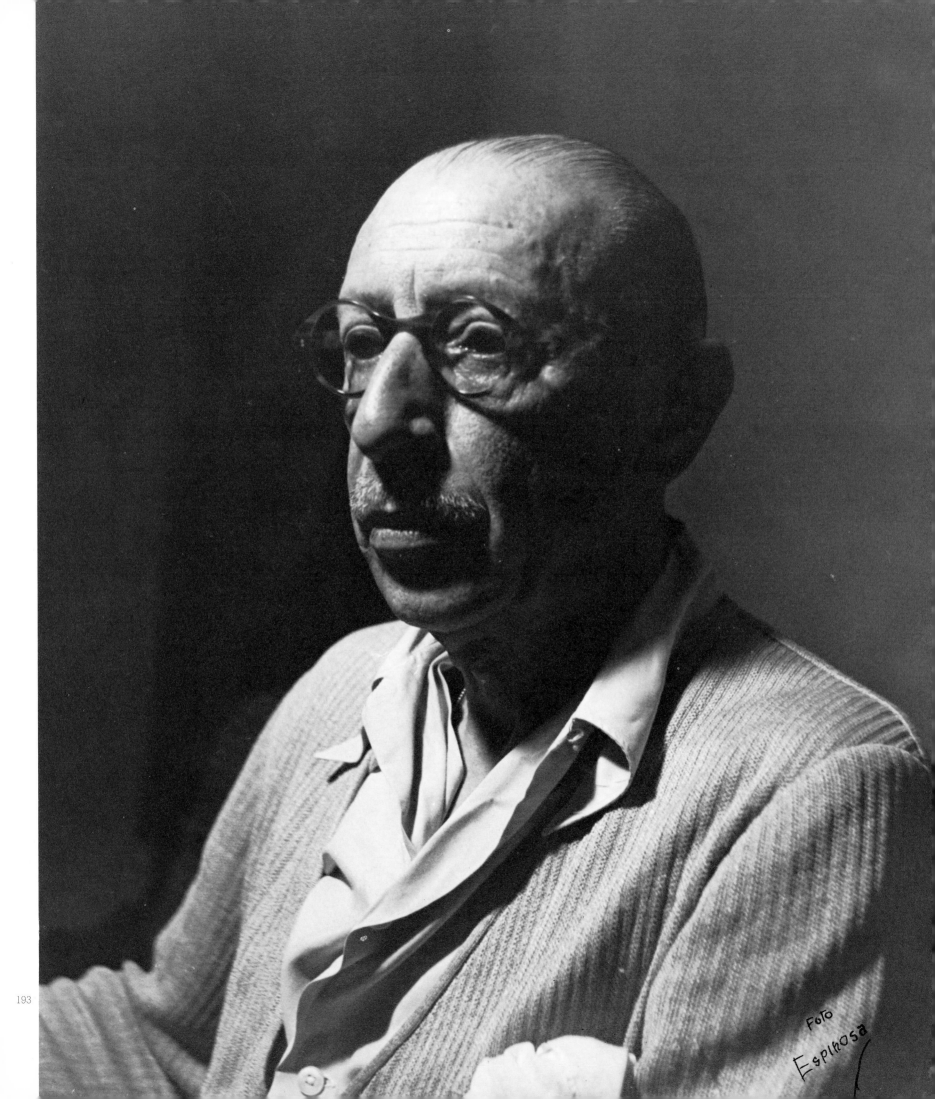

Foto
Espinosa

195 *June 1952*. Amsterdam. During a trip to Holland, the Stravinskys received a letter from Dr. Paul Cronheim of Amsterdam: "Cher maître et ami and Vera Carissima . . . Vera's dress at the concert in the Riddersaal in the Hague last night reminded me of the marvels that she made at the time of our *Carmen*, and also reminded me of our nocturnal walks in the little streets of the port of Amsterdam, the exquisite hours with Vera, Igor, and Mengelberg. I was moved to learn that you are in the Hôtel des Indes [in the Hague] where the great Diaghilev made a scandal with the concierge at 3 a.m. because the room of his *petit nègre* was not warm enough . . .'' (In Amsterdam, on March 17, 1928, Pierre Monteux had conducted the first performance of a new production of *Carmen* for which Vera had designed and made 300 costumes.)

196 *May 28, 1952*. Château de Laeken. With Queen Elizabeth of Belgium. On May 29, in Brussels, Stravinsky conducted *Scènes de Ballet* and *Oedipus Rex*. The Queen had invited Stravinsky to a performance of *Histoire du soldat* here on July 4, 1929, but he was in London and unable to attend.

In July 1957, the Queen, signing herself "votre très affectionnée Elizabeth," wrote to Stravinsky from the Château de Stuyvenberg asking him to compose a violin or piano concerto to be played by the contestants in her international competitions, 1959–60. (Stravinsky declined the invitation in a letter from Santa Fe, July 18, 1957.) Elizabeth's daughter, Marie-José, the ex-Queen of Italy, who lived in Geneva, was a good friend of Stravinsky's for many years. She published a tribute to him on his 80th birthday.

197 *Summer 1952*. On the front steps of 1260 North Wetherly Drive. Photograph by *Life* magazine.

194

196

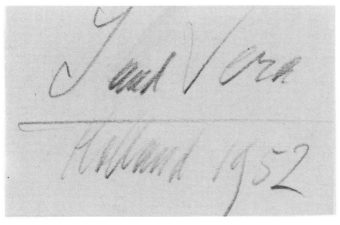

197

195

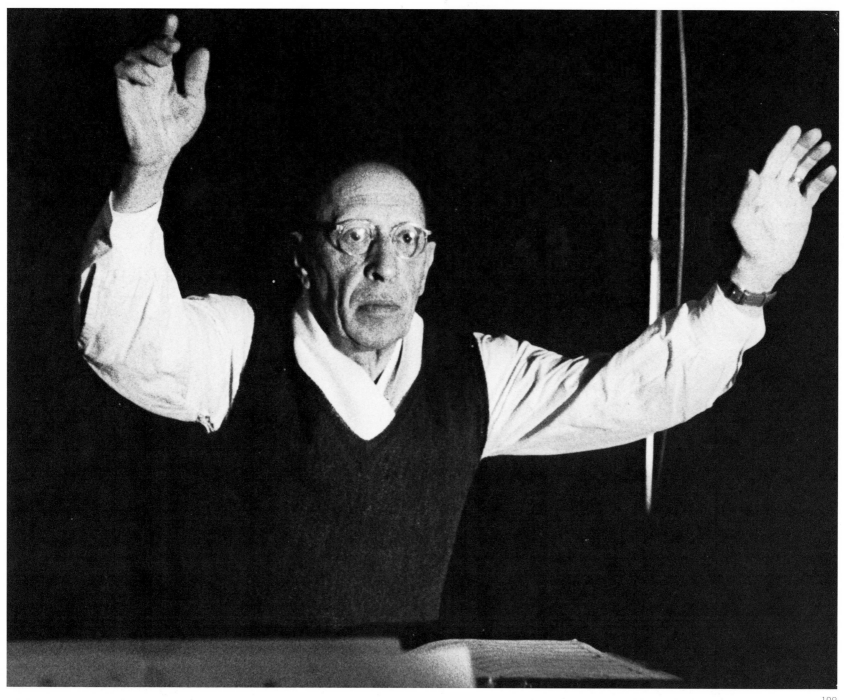

198 *May 1952.* Paris, Théâtre des Champs-Elysées. Rehearsing *Oedipus Rex.*

199 *December 1952.* "[As for] Stravinsky's workroom and working habits. . . . to achieve anything today, an artist has to develop a

conscious strictness in respect of time which in former ages might have seemed neurotic and selfish, for he must never forget that he is living in a state of siege. His workroom has also to be a fortress; the stopwatch and the metronome are his shield and buckler.

Similarly, howling storms, or a theatrical and purple artistic style [are] ridiculous [today], only clarity and economy will work as charms against the void. Intervals, as Stravinsky says, must be treated like dollars." (W. H. Auden, *The New York Times*, February 4, 1951)

200

200 *December 1952.* 1260 North Wetherly Drive. Vera is recovering from a thyroid operation. Igor is preparing to leave for concerts and recordings in Cleveland and New York.

201 *April 30, 1954.* On the train, Stresa to Geneva. Stravinsky had conducted in Rome on April 14 and 17 (*Orpheus, Scherzo à la Russe, Norwegian Moods, Circus Polka, Firebird* Suite), in Turin on the 23rd (*Ode*, the Violin Concerto—played by Jeanne Gautier— and *Perséphone* with Madeleine Milhaud as the narrator), and, on the 29th, with the radio orchestra of Monte-Ceneri in the Kursaal in Lugano (String Concerto, Septet, *Danses concertantes, Dumbarton Oaks* Concerto, *Pulcinella* Suite). According to a reporter from *Paris-Match*, during rehearsals Stravinsky "often interrupted his conducting to go into the hall . . . where he listened to the orchestra under its regular conductor. Once he said, 'La musique doit être souveraine.'"

202 *1954.* 1260 North Wetherly Drive.

201

203

204

205

206

203, 204, 205 *March 26, 1955.* Madrid. The day before, Stravinsky had conducted a concert consisting of the *Ode*, *Orpheus*, *Scènes de Ballet*, and the Symphony in Three Movements. On the 26th, the Stravinskys were at the Prado in the morning and in the Escurial (left) in the afternoon. They spent the evening with Ortega y Gasset. Far left, with the conductor, Ataulfo Argenta. Igor and Vera flew from Madrid to Rome on March 27. In Rome, on April 6, he conducted a concert of the *Ode*, Scene 3, Act I, *The Rake's Progress*, and *Oedipus Rex*. At the premiere of the

Rake, Eugenio Montale had likened Stravinsky, conducting, to ''a rubber puppet'' but also to ''Benedetto Croce bending over an ancient codex''. Unlike other commentators on the opera, the future Nobel Prize-winner noted that the stylistic diversity in the libretto (''*The Waste Land*, Gilbert and Sullivan'') became more coherent in the music.

206 *January 1956.* New York. Mirror photograph by and with Cecil Beaton, at the home, 11 East 77th Street, of Mme Lucia Davidova.

207

207 *January 1956*. New York. Photo by Cecil Beaton. Pavel Tchelichev's portrait of Mme Lucia Davidova is on the wall.

208 *September 1956*. Venice.

209 *September 1956*, Venice. The Lido. At the Film Festival. Mr. and Mrs. Arthur Rubinstein are in the row behind the Stravinskys.

208

209

210 *November 1956*. Munich. Photograph by
Herbert List.

211 *September 1956*. Venice. Looking at and
away from San Moisè.

212 *October 1956*. Munich. Red Cross
Hospital. With nurse Dagmar Senitza.
Stravinsky had suffered a major thrombosis
while conducting the Symphony in C in Berlin,
October 2, 1956.

213 *September 1957*. Venice. Stravinsky was
always restless sitting in an audience, and, as
Life magazine reported of him, he was known
to stand up and shout in protest when a piece
of his was being mauled. Dr. Maurice
Bernstein, a California friend, reported that he
was sitting next to Stravinsky in Hollywood
Bowl at a concert featuring one of his pieces,
and that Stravinsky constantly shook his head
"east to west and west to east, but never north
to south. When the playing and applause
were over, a sweet old lady seated directly
behind Stravinsky tapped him on the shoulder
and made bold to tell him that music of this
high character was not always appreciated at
first: 'In time you would learn . . . to enjoy the
higher forms of musical literature. I suggest
you become a subscriber to the concerts.'
Stravinsky, always a gentleman, answered:
'I'll try it, if it kills me.'" (*Chicago Herald
American*, January 12, 1944.)

211

213

212

214

214 *September 1957*. Venice. Photograph by Marvin Koner, CBS Records.

215 *September 21, 1957*. Venice. With Giorgio de Chirico.

216 *June 1958*. Hollywood. Recording the *Symphony of Psalms*.

215

217

218

219

217, 218 *September 1958.* (**218**) wall in Venice. The premiere of *Threni* took place on September 23; Vera's exhibition at the Cavallino Gallery opened a few days earlier. In the photo above (**217**), Igor is helping Vera to hang her paintings.

219 *April 11, 1959.* Tokyo. On April 11, Stravinsky wrote to his son Theodore: "Tokyo, in my impression, is not interesting at all; an immense city with horrible streets and no architecture . . . We are impatiently awaiting Kyoto, the ancient capital . . . We leave tomorrow, Miyako Hotel, and stay for 12 days. We are here again on the 23rd. Vera's exhibition is the 24th and from the 25th to the 30th I have two rehearsals a day (Bob will help me, otherwise it would be too tiring). On the 30th we go to Osaka, where my first concert takes place on May 1. On the 2nd, we return here, where I conduct on the 3rd and 7th."

220 *1959.* 1260 North Wetherly Drive. With Gerald Heard. Photograph by Michael Barrie.

221 *1958.* T.S. Eliot's dedication to Vera in a copy of *Old Possum's Book of Practical Cats.*

222 *September 1959.* Torcello. Photograph by Richard Hammond.

220

to
Igor
Madame Stravinsky
in memory of a very
happy evening
T.S. Eliot
9.xii.58

221

222

223

224

223 *September 1, 1960.* Buenos Aires. Photograph by Victoria Ocampo, in her San Isidro home.

224 *September 22, 1960.* Rome. Photograph from *The Daily American.* The Stravinskys were driven from Ciampino Airport to a hotel in Perugia. They spent most of the next day at Borgo San Sepolcro, looking at the paintings by Piero della Francesca, but also visited Gubbio, reaching Venice late at night.

225 *September 30, 1961.* Belgrade Airport. Brigitta Lieberson (Vera Zorina), ribbon in hair, sits across the table from the Stravinskys.

225

Nuoruuden hauskoja muistoja Helsingistä, Imatralta ja Viipurin lie-
peiltä. Myös rouva Stravinski on käynyt Kannaksella vuosia sit-
ten. Molemmat ovat kosmopoliitteja ja iloisia maailmanmatkaajia.

Caj Bremer

226

227

226 *September 15, 1961.* Helsinki. Photo from
Vikko, No. 37.

227 *November 9, 1961.* Kingsford Smith
Airport, Sydney, Australia. After a nine-day
"vacation" touring Egypt, the Stravinskys had
flown from Cairo to Karachi, Calcutta,
Bangkok, Singapore, Darwin, and Sydney.
After one day in the Australian city, they flew
to Auckland, and, after a concert there, to
Wellington. On November 21, they were back
in Sydney for a concert, on November 24 in
Melbourne for a concert. On the 29th they
flew to Tahiti, via Sydney, the New Hebrides,
and the Fiji Islands. On December 7, Igor and
Vera flew to Los Angeles and on the 17th to
Mexico City.

228 *November 1961.* Arrival at Tahiti from
Australia, 2 a.m.

228

Al Teatro Massimo il più grande musicista vivente

Stasera concerto di Igor Strawinsky

229 *January 18, 1962.* At the White House. By an extraordinary coincidence this photograph appeared in a newspaper in Catania on November 22, 1963, *before* the news of the assassination had reached Italy. On November 23, *"il più grande musicista vivente"* conducted his Mass in the President's memory.

On a visit to Washington in December 1960, Mme Stravinsky had given an interview published under the title "To Wife of Composer-Conductor Stravinsky Washington is Pianissimo":

"Vera Stravinsky, wife of the famous composer, is a very well-travelled woman. 'Just ask me about it,' she suggested, her voice challenging during an interview in the Jefferson Hotel yesterday afternoon. 'It's frightful. This packing and unpacking all the time—and all the time finding the wrong dress' . . . Turning to Washington, she said, 'You know, life is terrible here, you drink too much, you eat too much . . . What is the matter here that they don't dress? In South America it was lovely—everybody looking splendid. But here they wear sweaters to opening night.'

"Mme. Stravinsky has found Washington a little on the quiet side, a quality she doesn't especially admire in cities. 'Quietness you create yourself in your house, if you want it. But here, on Christmas Day, my birthday, and

a big day for us, we [want] a little bit of champagne. Did you ever try to get champagne here on Christmas Day? Impossible! Everything is closed and instead of parties I had to put my coat on and rush to find a restaurant open.'" (*The Washington Post*, December 31, 1960)

GUEST LEAVES WHITE HOUSE EARLY
President and Mrs. Kennedy celebrated the end of their first year in the White House yesterday by giving a small private dinner Thursday in honor of the great Russian-born composer-conductor Igor Stravinsky and his wife. But the musician, weary after a day of rehearsals for the production of his *Oedipus Rex*, had to leave the party early . . . Guests had come from London, Paris, New York and Chicago . . .

Mrs. Kennedy and the President walked outside the door of the Diplomat Room and stood in the cold without wraps as the Stravinskys got out of the White House car sent to conduct them to the party.

Mrs. Stravinsky said that the evening had given her husband and herself the greatest pleasure and was a very great honor among all the honors her husband has received. "But he is not as young as he once was," she said. "He rehearsed today and has to get up early to rehearse again tomorrow." Mrs. Stravinsky was seated at President Kennedy's right at the

oval table in the state dining room. She and the President sat midway down the table's length, rather than at the end. They faced the First Lady and Stravinsky across the table.

Mrs. Kennedy's sister, Lee Radziwill, was there, with a friend, Princess Chavchavadze. Mr. and Mrs. Marshall Field had come from Chicago. From New York came Leonard Bernstein and his lovely wife. Special Assistant to the President and Mrs. Arthur Schlesinger, Jr., and Mrs. Salinger were in the group. The Stravinskys came with the composer's co-conductor Robert Craft.

After dinner, Mrs. Kennedy led the women into the newly redecorated Red Room and the President took the men into the Green Room—all except for Stravinsky. A devoted husband, he followed right along after his handsome wife into the Red Room. The men stayed briefly by themselves. As soon as they joined the ladies, Stravinsky went up to Mrs. Kennedy and made his excuses. She graciously insisted that he leave since she knew he had a difficult day ahead of him.

(*The Washington Post*, January 19, 1962.)

230 *March 1962.* In his new library. On May 15, 1960, Stravinsky made an arrangement of the "Lullaby" from *The Rake's Progress* for two recorders, a gift for the architect who had designed this room and built these bookshelves.

231

232

233

234

231 *March 31, 1962.* Hollywood. CBS Studios. Studying *The Flood* before dressing to be filmed. Photograph by Ernst Haas.

232 *June 15, 1962.* Hamburg. Arriving for the Stravinsky 80th birthday festival at the Hamburg Opera. The New York City Ballet performed *Orpheus* (conducted by Leopold Ludwig), *Agon* (conducted by Robert Craft), and *Apollo* (conducted by Stravinsky).

233 *June 18, 1962.* The silver frame and photographs were given to Stravinsky on his 80th birthday by Mr. and Mrs. Goddard Lieberson.

234–237 *June 18, 1962.* Hamburg. Honored on his 80th birthday by the Mayor, Senator and some distinguished citizens of Hamburg, Stravinsky received a first edition of Lessing. The composer's speech was the work of Vera (who wrote most of Stravinsky's German-language letters for him).

"Herr Bürgermeister, Herr Senator, Meine Damen und Herren, Ich möchte etwas sagen, was mir in Gedanken und am Herzen liegt: dass ein berühmtes deutsches Theater eine berühmte Ballet Truppe engagiert um ein Stravinsky Abend dem Publikum anzubieten ist *unglaublich, undenkbar* in andern Ländern—nur in Deutschland kann so etwas passieren, wo die Kultur der Musik Jahrhunderte lang gepflegt wird. Vielen, vielen Dank."

235

237

236

238 *August 29, 1962.* Lod Airport, Israel. Greeted by Aaron Propes, who directed the Festival of Israel.

239 *September 21, 1962.* Arriving in Moscow.. Aeroflot.

240 *October 1962.* Leningrad. Dinner at the Composers' Union. The man on Stravinsky's right is Vladimir Nikolayevich Rimsky-Korsakov, son of the composer.

241 On October 11, 1962, the Stravinskys flew in an Air France Caravelle from Moscow to Paris (Orly), and on October 12 *Humanité* published a report telegraphed from Moscow by Max Léon, of an interview with Stravinsky at the airport:

"Before leaving the U.S.S.R., after three weeks of a triumphant tour, Igor Stravinsky was received for one hour by Nikita Khrushchev . . . 'Nikita Sergeivich invited me to return for a vacation in the Crimea or the Caucasus. He talked to me about very interesting development projects that he had inspected on a tour of Central Asia . . . What an extraordinary man. He asked me to tell him very frankly what I did not find good during my tour, what disappointed me most. I was very embarrassed, of course, but after a moment I said: "I was obliged to drink a little too much vodka."'

"'What souvenirs of the U.S.S.R. are you taking with you?'

"'A bottle of vodka, but I will drink it slowly.'

"'Leningrad is the most beautiful city not only in the U.S.S.R., but in all Europe. We gave six concerts with twelve rehearsals—which is not much rehearsing, considering that I did not know the orchestras. The work was very agreeable, which is also the opinion of my friend Robert Craft, who was with me.'

"'Did you speak of any musical projects with Nikita Khrushchev?'

"'Yes, but we agreed to keep the secret between ourselves.'"

     *   *   *

From an interview at Orly Airport by Jacqueline Leulliot:

"I discovered Moscow with great emotion. I had never seen it—I spent only four hours there sixty years ago—and I am eighty years old. It is a very animated city, full of beautiful things. . . . I was happy to see St. Petersburg again, and the place where I was born, and to see it all in autumnal splendour . . . My niece in Leningrad is a grandmother now and her three-year-old grandchild has the name Igor.

134

238

239

"The Russian audiences are very touching . . . I forgot that I am a musician before I talked to Khrushchev about his recent trip in Central Asia. I found him in magnificent spirits . . ."

      *   *   *

Michel Gordey, another Orly reporter, wrote: "The 1958 edition of the *Grande Encyclopédie Soviétique* (51 large volumes) does not mention his name . . . Vera Stravinskaya, his wife, stood by his side with her arms full of flowers. He said: 'In Leningrad in the old Hall of the Nobles, I told the audience, "You see that corner over there, in the balcony. I sat there with my mother sixty-eight years ago, at the concert commemorating the death of the great composer Tchaikovsky. I never believed that I would return in my life. But here I am."'"

242 *November 9, 1962.* Caracas. With American Ambassador Stewart and his wife in their residence, "La Florida."

240

De retour d'U.R.S.S. où il a donné 6 concerts
IGOR STRAVINSKY A PARIS : *A 81 ans, je viens de découvrir Moscou*

241

Recepción en la Embajada Norteamericana
En Honor de Igor Stravinsky y Señora

242

135

243 *June 3, 1963*. Dublin. Signing autographs. A week before this photo was taken, the Stravinskys had visited David (*In Parenthesis*, *The Anathemata*) Jones, in Harrow. He later described the couple in a letter:

"I was greatly honored . . . by a visit at Whitsuntide by Stravinsky and his wife . . . They were absolutely sweet, both of them, straightforward, direct, appreciative, amusing and relaxed . . . it was a jolly nice visit" (September 16, 1963).

"You say I am a classic. But what does that mean? I am accepted by some musicians, maybe even by a great many, and I have been widely honored. But the ignorance of critics is so obvious to the musician, that one cannot ignore it. I have no choice but to say this, to draw attention to it. You find bad composers and bad pianists, full of vindictiveness, writing criticism. My eightieth birthday was last year. Many events were arranged, I was invited everywhere, tributes were paid—except in the American newspapers, one of which was so abusive that I sent a letter telling them: 'Are . . . you not ashamed to have as music critic one whose knowledge of music is so low? [P. H. Lang of the *New York Herald Tribune*] I regret only that [being] eighty years old, I have very little hope of celebrating his funeral.' They wrote back asking me if they could publish the letter. I told them it had already been published—in Germany . . .

"We have to know our time and what is happening in it. We must be able to feel how periods change. For instance, I was in Russia last year . . . invited by the Government, and everyone was very hospitable. But their musical life is stuck fast in the nineteenth century. There is nothing new that I can learn there . . . I am in key with the Russian—sub-Russian—origins of my music. But I certainly belong to the modern Western spirit rather than to that of the nineteenth-century romantic composers whom the Russians especially like . . . *Le Sacre* had a very big influence on the music of the period and even up to the present. But we have new problems to resolve now. Harmonic problems—rhythmic problems—it is hard to express them in words. You speak about Bach, but there were very great composers before Bach. If they are not played, it is mainly because people do not know how to play them. Bach is closer to us because we can perform him. But 'who is greater, Bach or Beethoven?' has no sense as a question. You might as well ask if one breed of dog is greater than another."

(From an interview with Brian Fallon, *The Irish Times*, June 8, 1963)

244 *June 7, 1963*. Dublin. With Eamon de Valera. Photo from the *Evening Herald*.

245 *October 1964*. Berlin.

246 *June 28, 1965*. Muncie, Indiana, photographed in the Red Lion Room at the Van Orman-Roberts Hotel.

Being the wife of a world-renowned . . . musical genius is easy if you know how. "Sometimes I'm good to him, sometimes I'm grouchy, and when he writes something I don't understand, I just smile and tell him 'It's wonderful.'" So says Madame Igor Stravinsky sipping gin and tonic. She had just come in from a brief shopping trip to the nearest corner drugstore to pick up something on which to sketch a rug design. She's going to make a rug for her home in Beverly Hills, California. She's a painter.

"My art work is pure fantasy," she told us. "This rug is going to be a Capricorn design." Madame Stravinsky is a Capricorn, born on Christmas Day 50 to 60 years ago, probably. "We always celebrate Christmas in the morning and my birthday in the evening," she laughingly admitted, and then dropped the subject. She's attractive, vivacious, fluent in four-and-a-half languages and as much at home in Europe as in America . . .

The three days and five nights the Stravinskys are in Muncie this week for the Ball State University Festival of Arts are the first they've had in a small midwestern city. Their stops in this part of the U.S. have been in the big cities, Chicago, Cleveland, Cincinnati. Now they are visiting grass-roots America.

Some of what they've seen is puzzling. "We drove from Indianapolis (their plane landed at Weir Cook Airport) and we saw all these nice homes along the way with their big lawns, but we didn't see many people . . . no children playing, no one sitting out front visiting . . . no lights on in most of the houses. Where are the people?"

Big lawns bother Madame Stravinsky. "[They are] just to impress the neighbors. In California we have just moved to our new home and it has a big, green lawn. [Either] it's just been watered—and water is so expensive in California and it takes so much for the lawns—or just been fertilized, and sometimes the fertilizer doesn't smell very good. I got tired of this. Anyway, I'd always wanted a garden full of flowers, so I gave the gardener a picture of an English garden and told him I wanted flowers. Now we have such a garden. Flowers everywhere with little paths of brick so you can get around in it, and admire them. Now I have something I can enjoy too."

*   *   *

. . . "What's Stravinsky's reaction if he's sitting in a concert and the performance isn't particularly good?" we asked.

Madame Igor Stravinsky, the "audience reactor" for her husband's music, gets the usual husband's tribute. "If she likes it the audience will."—Evening Press Photo.

246

"He doesn't go to many concerts."

"What if it's his own music and he's obligated?"

"Well, then, if it isn't very good he sits there very dignified and showing nothing of what he thinks."

"What do you do when you don't enjoy a concert?"

"I go to sleep. Sometimes I snore. One time there was a little scandal in Paris because I went to sleep during a concert."

Another flurry of gossip occurred in Belgium when Madame Stravinsky turned down an invitation to have lunch with the Queen of Belgium. "There were other things I had to do and I just couldn't," she told us. "Later my friends all told me you can't turn down an invitation from Her Majesty. I told them 'I can, I'm an American . . .'" (From the *Muncie Evening Press*, June 31, 1965)

247 *September 1965*. Frankfurt. En route New York–Hamburg.

248 *January 1967*. New York. Stravinsky's drawing, after Edward Lear.

247

The Owl and the Pussy-Cat
to Vera

Igor Stravinsky

249 *June 1966*. Paris, Grand Vefour. Photograph by Henri Cartier-Bresson.

250 *Spring 1967*. 1218 North Wetherly Drive (the Stravinskys' address from the autumn of 1964). Photograph by Claudio Spies.

251 *November 1969*. New York, Essex House. Photograph by Richard Avedon.

252 *August 24, 1970*. Evian. Photo by Lord Snowdon.

253 *August 1970*. Evian. Photo by Vera.

254 *Christmas 1970*. New York, Essex House.

249

250

251

252

253

254

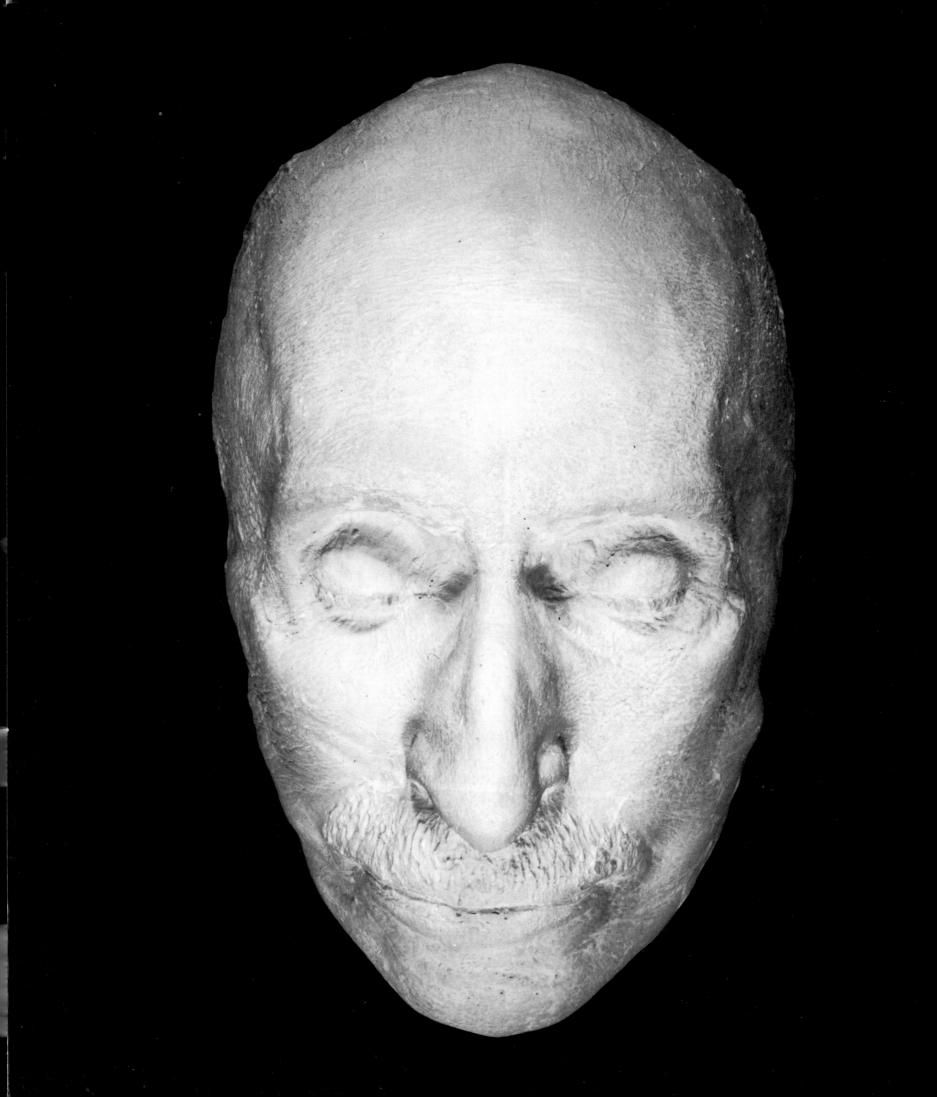

256

257

255 *April 6, 1971.* In this death mask, the lines from the oxygen tubes are still visible.

256, 257 *August 1975.* San Michele. In an interview with Lesley Thornton in *Harper's & Queen Magazine*, London, October 1979), Vera is quoted as follows: ''When I was in trouble I would talk to him. He always gave me the right answer to a problem, a very short answer. I'd ask him 'What shall I do?' and he told me. Yes, I miss him very much.

''At the last minute I was there . . . he had such strength, I thought, tomorrow he will be all right . . .''

Thornton added: ''Vera misses Stravinsky every day and all the time. But there is no sign of self-pity in her. It does not seem likely that there ever has been. Her acceptance of the past has nothing to do with the resignation of age or memory blurred.''

"It must be said that Mme Stravinsky has glamour. We met in her suite at the Dorchester. She was over from New York, where she now lives, to attend the premiere of Covent Garden's recent production of *The Rake's Progress* [June 18, 1979]. She sat upright, ignoring the soft invitation of the pillowed sofa back; her shapely arms and hands moved as she talked in gestures which showed the influence of her early ballet training. She wore flowing chiffon and curls, jewelry, peeptoe sandals and varnished toenails. She speaks unaffectedly, with a pleasingly Russian turn of phrase and accent. One of the most striking and appealing things about her is that she seems quite untouched by the legendary treatment she is accorded: people appear much more impressed by her than she is by herself.

"She and Stravinsky, Vera said, were very alike. 'We had the same kind of education in Russia. We were both born in St. Petersburg . . . We knew each other's troubles.' Madame was interviewed on television in Paris about an exhibition of her paintings which was about to open there. [One] question was, 'Didn't Stravinsky want you to be a musician so that you could criticize his work?' 'Monsieur,' she said, 'you know, in order to criticize a genius you must have genius.' Madame commented drily that it is really the last thing a genius wants, someone sitting around the house criticizing. 'He liked me, musician or not musician,' she said, smiling. Madame has always enjoyed life. 'Yesterday I had lunch at the Ritz with friends, Isaiah Berlin and Stephen Spender were there. I sat next to Isaiah Berlin and we told stories, we laughed terribly. I am not young any more. But I still enjoy life. Something bad, I push it away.'"
(Lesley Thornton, *Harper's & Queen Magazine*, London, October 1979.)

258 At the Covent Garden premiere of *The Rake's Progress*, the most astonishing event of the evening occurred in the first scene of the third act. Baba the Turk removes her wedding ring at one point, and, in this production, flings it into the audience. On this occasion the thin, gold band landed in the lap of Vera Stravinsky, no doubt directed there by Igor Stravinsky himself, on this, his birthday, since the singer did not know where Mrs Stravinsky was sitting, and, in any case, could not in a thousand conscious attempts have hit this target.

258